Dr FEGG's
ENCYCLOPEADIA OF ALL
WORLD KNOWLEDGE

CONGRATULATIONS

BARNSLEY TOWN HALL

BARNSLEY

You have won ... and ask them to wrap it
Go to ... and ask them to wrap it
up for you. If there is any trouble, like: 'Do
you realize there are 3,000 people working
in here?' just show them your copy of
Dr Fegg's Encyclopeadia of All World
Knowledge (formerly The Nasty Book)
[If they still refuse to wrap the building up for yo
there's nothing much you can do.]

The ONLY book to give a public building away with every copy

Dr BERTRAM X. FEGG G.B.H. (Parkhurst)
— A living educational legend —
*'Bring the little ones unto me, and I will get
a good price for them'*

Dr FEGG's ENCYCLOPEADIA OF <u>ALL</u> WORLD KNOWLEDGE

(formerly THE NASTY BOOK)

TERRY JONES & MICHAEL PALIN

Peter Bedrick Books
New York

OTHER BOOKS BY DR FEGG

The Bournemouth Killings – An Explanation
The Bournemouth Toe-Nailings – What Really Happened
Where I was on the Night of the Twenty-sixth
Why I have Never Even Been to Bournemouth
The Bournemouth Killings – Another Version
Innocent Until Proved Guilty
Great Alibis of the Twentieth Century

For Children

The Bournemouth Killings – A Frame-Up
I-Spy The Police

New revised edition. First published
in the United States 1985 by Peter
Bedrick Book, NY. *Bert Fegg's Nasty
Book for Boys and Girls* first published
1974 by Eyre Methuen Ltd. This edition
published by agreement with Methuen
London Ltd.

Copyright © 1974, 1976 and 1984 by Terry Jones and Michael Palin

Designed by James Campus

Illustrated by Martin Honeysett
Also by Kai Choi, Ken Cox, Martin Handford, Dennis Hawkins, Roy Ingram,
Sally Ingram, Robin MacFarlan, Strat Mastoris, Mike Spiller

Photographs courtesy of John Cleare, Mary Evans Picture Library,
Eddie Jones, Keystone Press Agency, Pan Am,
Photographers' Library, Popperfoto, Quadrant Picture Library,
Sport and General Press Agency, Syndication International and
United Press International

Library of Congress Cataloging in Publication Data

Jones, Terry.
  Dr. Fegg's encyclopeadia of all world knowledge:
(formerly The nasty book)

  Rev. ed. of: Bert Fegg's nasty book for boys and
girls. 1974.
  Summary: An illustrated compendium of humorous facts
such as the recipe for oxygen tart and an explanation
of how man evolved from small rocks.
  1. English wit and humor. 2. Wit and humor, Juvenile.
[1. Wit and humor] I. Palin, Michael. II. Jones,
Terry. Bert Fegg's nasty book for boys and girls.
III, Title. IV. Title: Doctor Fegg's encyclopeadia of all
world knowledge.
PN6175.J66 1985 828'.91402 84-24479
ISBN 0-87226-005-4 (pbk.)

DELIFERATE MISTALE

Bsoy and Girls! Somewhat in this blok, thre is a deliferate mistale. It
may be a pocture or a world or ever the pange gumbers could be
wrong. If you cal spot the DELIFERATE MISTALE, write to the
Weditor, and you will delieve £24,000 by returb of nost.

CONTENTS

S

T

U

V

W

X

Y

Z

PUBLISHER'S FOREWORD

We should like to take this opportunity of assuring you that there is absolutely no truth in the rumour that Dr Fegg has at any time been in jail. Dr Fegg's police record is spotless. He has, of course, had the usual parking offences, but these are *not criminal offences*; they are only *civil misdemeanours*. Dr Fegg has never done 'bird', nor was he in any way connected with the petty thefts and larcenies in Brighton three months ago, although the circumstances were admittedly rather against him; but HE WAS NOT CONVICTED! We want to emphasise that – and don't forget: a man is entirely innocent until he is CONVICTED. And he's never even been *charged* with the Bournemouth killings, and anyway, they *were* a long time ago.

We are proud to publish this book. There is no question of us doing it because we are 'running scared' or 'don't want to lose any authors in nasty accidents' or are afraid of getting our noses 'spread all over our faces'. Oh no, we at Methuen are committed to the book, to its author, and to his continuing struggle to prove his innocence.

Methuen London

WARNING
This book features many of the less savoury aspects of human behaviour. But you have been warned. We believe that it is far better we should face reality, however horrible, than stick our heads, sand-like, into an ostrich. Thank you.

APOLOGY
We apologise for making such a mess of the metaphor above. It should, of course, read 'than head-first stick sand in an ostrich'. Thank you.

ANATOMY (The Human Body)
The body comes in two parts. The top part and the bottom part. These two parts are usually joined together by the "middle" making three parts altogether, so the start of this paragraph is quite wrong. In certain cases however this may be missing (*see* Magic: *Sawing The Lady In Half*).

THE HUMAN BODY

The Top Half

THE NOSE

The top half of the body is organized so that it is *behind* the nose. This is important because if you're going to hit someone you might as well hit the bit that's nearest, and that's usually the nose – unless they have their back to you in which case you can take your pick – especially if you creep up on them.

THE HEAD

Immediately behind the nose is the head. Heads aren't much good for anything really except putting in a box and forgetting about.

They're too heavy to play football with, and tend to frighten off visitors if stuck over the front door. (Also a head over your door is an open invitation to the merciless hounds of the law.)

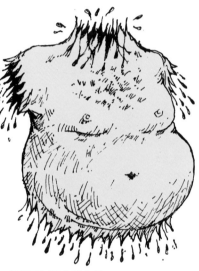

THE TORSO

This is definitely the heaviest bit. It fills an entire suitcase and practically pulls your arm off. Best to get a trolley if you're travelling any distance with a torso. And don't keep your sandwiches in the same suitcase, otherwise you might get a few odd glances when every time you go to eat your lunch, it's like opening the Jonathan Miller pop-up book. Also, if anyone *does* ask you what you've got in the case – keep off the mother-in-law jokes and just hit them (*see* 'Nose' above).

THE ARM

Strictly speaking there should be two arms but I lost one. All right! *You* try carrying two suitcases, one hat box and a carrier bagful 200 miles without dropping a few bits, especially when you've got to avoid the ticket collector as well! It's lucky I didn't lose any of the legs.

The Bottom Half

THE LEG

All right! I *did* mislay one of the legs as well, but it could've happened to anyone. I mean, *you* try dragging all that luggage with you every time you need to go to the toilet to avoid the ticket inspector!

THE LEFT FOOT

This is the one to be careful of. Nothing is easier than to *think* you've got the whole lot packed, only to find the left foot is dangling out of the side, frightening all the kiddies.

REMEMBER,

the Human Body is a wonderful thing, and it deserves a decent-sized suitcase.

ANIMALS

In all the Wonderful World of Nature, animals are the most fascinating of God's creations. Here are a few specially selected for *Dr Fegg's Encyclopeadia of All World Knowledge.*

The Ferocious Amazonian Killer Skunk

Perhaps the most unpleasant animal in the whole of the Wonderful World. Can spot its victim from distance of up to fifty miles, charge at a speed of seventy mph, apply its bottom to its victim's nose, and produce a lethal fart, to which there is no known antidote.

This animal can find you wherever you are, as it can read phone directories or even get in touch with your bank.

The 'Montana' Boiling Tiger

Placed in a pan of boiling water for ten minutes, this tiger makes a delicious lunch snack. Garnish with sweet corn and dill cucumbers.

Bengali Bomber Ant

This extremely dangerous and unpredictable termite is capable of flying Lancaster Bombers, Spitfires, and even Sabre jets at speeds well in excess of Mach one. Indeed, such is its success at getting performances out of obsolete combat aircraft, far above their technical specifications, that an independent board of enquiry has been attached to the War Office to learn some of the Bomber Ant's secrets. At present, the main objective of the enquiry is to get near enough to the Ant's heavily defended strategic HQ to be able to make contact via the Red Cross or some independent body covered by the Geneva Convention.

The Ready-To-Eat Fish from South Dakota

This slow-moving, dull-witted creature is so-called because it contains mashed potato, peas, carrots and a warm plate inside its body. Protests feebly when eaten.

The Turkish Wall Goat

Unfortunately incontinent, the Turkish Wall Goat is a constant hazard on the streets of Ankara. Its ability to climb any vertical surface and remain there for many weeks on end has rendered some side streets virtually impassable. Perhaps the worst feature of this antisocial animal is its habit of shouting at young women and making misleading statements to the press about the present Turkish government.

The Lighter-than-Air Otter

This is one of the few dirigible otters in the Western Free World. A politically irresponsible animal, it produces a strange whooping noise when released, but refuses to see a doctor. The otter will keep in a refrigerator for up to five minutes, or two minutes in the ice compartment.

The Patagonian Bursting Rabbit

This extremely dangerous rodent eats up to six times its own weight in food, refuse, and old copies of *The Watchtower*. It then lies in wait for its prey, disguised as the comparatively harmless Patagonian Shoe-Cleaning Rat (*see separate entry*) and, upon contact with the victim's shoe, explodes with the force of twenty pounds of TNT, covering the victim in an unpleasant mixture of predigested food and evangelical magazines.

The Argentinian Leaping Cow and Badger

Distantly related to the Squatting Pig and Mongoose, this interesting animals is found only in Scotland and Fiji, and lives solely on a diet of ants and milk. During the leaping season, which lasts for four hours, thousands of these happy creatures get sucked into aircraft engines.

The Californian Thinking Lizard

There are few sights more unnerving in the whole of the Wonderful World than the sight of this lizard thinking. It thinks about everything: whether to get up, whether to walk backwards or forwards – it even thinks about whether to stand still or not. Unfortunately, although it thinks so much, the lizard is incapable of coming to any decisions, and has to survive off tiny insects that crawl into its mouth and wander down into its stomach. And, even then, many of them just walk out again.

The Patagonian Shoe-Cleaning Rat

Perhaps the most harmless and least offensive animal in existence. This rat lives by hiring itself out as a shoe brush. Once it goes bald, its career is at an end, and it has to rely on what it can make out of selling Patagonian Rat's Cheese (which, understandably, isn't very popular).*

The West Bromley Fighting Haddock

An all too increasing phenomenon around West Bromley nowadays – especially at closing time – is this violent and abusive Fighting Haddock. It is usually found hanging round the door of the Public Bar ready to attack defenceless members of Parliament, vicars, and gaming-club owners. Its rough manners and disgusting language have made the Fighting Haddock feared throughout the Bromley area and the South-East.

*This animal really needs all the help it can get, so if you have any contributions, send them to:

  Help the Patagonian Shoe-Cleaning Rat Fund
  c/o The Lubrication Bay
  "El Diablo" Shell Garage Buenos Aires

The Argentinian Leaping
Cow and Badger

The Ready-To-Eat Fish
from South Dakota

The Turkish Wall Goat

The West Bromley
Fighting Haddock

The Patagonian
Shoe-Cleaning Rat

The Lighter-than-Air Otter

The Californian Thinking Lizard

The 'Montana'
Boiling Tiger

The Patagonian
Bursting Rabbit

The Ferocious Amazonian Killer Skunk

Bengali Bomber Ant

ANTHEMS

Dr Fegg has only ever written one national anthem. Here it is, reproduced in full for the first time. Dr Fegg would like to remind all his readers that he has not yet been paid for it.

The Gambian National Anthem

Gambia, Oh Gambia,
Though only small and thin,
When it comes to being called
   Gambia,
You are the one to win.

Your capital is Bathurst
A name that means so much,
To you who live in Gambia,
Though less so to the Dutch.

Gambia, where men are men
And trees fit in the ground.
The one six-lettered nation
Where Gambians abound!

Gambians! O Gambians!
Though your country is so thin
And most of it a river
It's the place that you live in.

BIOGRAPHY

A biography is a book about someone slightly more interesting than the author, except in the case of Dr Fegg's biography, in which the subject of the book is so vastly more interesting than any snivelling, cross-eyed scribbler that it just doesn't bear thinking about. Anyway, this is it.

AN EXTRACT FROM THE LIFE OF Dr FEGG

EURGGGGH!

From mountains down to flat
bits,
Ring out your anthem great,
Though now you're part of
Senegal
The words are out of date.

Bertram Wesley Fegg DD

WARNING: Humming of this anthem,
even to oneself, renders the reader liable
for royalty payments. These should be sent
to Dr Fegg personally and *not*, repeat *not*
to the black chisellers at the Gambian
embassy.

CHICKENS

Recent laboratory tests at the Institute of Advanced Chickenish Research have revealed that the chicken has a far more advanced and sophisticated brain than was once thought, and may be man's greatest ally in the feathered world, beating even the famous Esoteric Ducks of the Hooghly River, and making the Gannet who put together a Nesting Bird's edition of Shelley seem almost dim.

According to Dr Rex Bantam, experiments have shown that the 'cluck-cluck' noise emitted by chickens, when replayed on a tape 1400 times slower than normal speed, reveals that the chicken is in fact saying. 'Can I have some more pellets do you think? Can I have some more

pellets do you think?' and some cockerels are actually reciting poetry. In another amazing experiment, the common or garden egg was analysed under a micronoscope and found to contain an amazingly sophisticated yellow computerised early warning system. 'Each egg yolk could save man thirty or forty million pounds', claimed the head of the Institute, Dr Hans Schaefer, who is himself a Rhode Island Red. He asked for more money to be spent on chicken research and could he have some more pellets do you think?

(Information from *Chickens, Man's Best Friend*, by Basil D'Oliveira)

PART ONE: THE BEGINNING

It was a HORRI-BLE night! Trees fell to the ground! The Wind was like a rhinoceros! Each Flash of Lightning lasted an hour! And in the stinking hovel where Mr and Mrs Fegg did their dark deeds which no one dared talk about, there was a wail and a roar! A scream, so loud you could see it, hurtled out of the chimney! There was a crash so loud that the roof flew off, and *aaaaarrrrgh!* HORRORS! Fegg was born!

His parents took one look at him and fled.

Fegg grabbed an axe and smashed down the door! *Grrrrr!*

Smelt burning

An Inspector of Inland Waterways, who was combing his hair in a boat smelt burning. It was the grass burning under Bert Fegg's feet as he ran along the bank, landed in the boat, and threw out the Inspector into the cold, old water of the river Thames. The boat was seen from a lighthouse rowing head-on into the

Westerlies at a speed of 300 miles per hour! Fegg was angry!

Fegg rowed to Orkney, where he found his parents doing their dark deeds that nobody dared talk about, and he taught them a lesson! He knotted his mother's knickers and he bent his father's pipe and he put marmalade in their shoes. They were sorry they'd ever had him.

Then Fegg asked if he had any brothers or sisters and they said he had a brother in catering somewhere in Kent. So he knocked a policeman off his bicycle and cycled away so fast that the road behind him turned to molten tar and all the cars and pedestrians got stuck in it.

Fegg got to the sea and swore so loudly that the fish came up to see and he cycled across right on their heads. And he got to Scotland and came so fast that the motorway curled up behind him.

When he found his brother making flapjacks in Kent, he punched him on the nose and put his socks through the mincer. Oh, he was sorry he had a brother like Bert!

Then Bert Fegg looked around him and saw a lady in a hat. He was so angry! He hit her hat off her head and bit her arm and then kicked a soldier and took an axe and wrecked a bus.

The Mayor and Corporation met to decide what should be done. But before they'd finished meeting, Fegg came and jumped on the table, and he tied their chains of office in knots and pushed their hats over their heads and rolled all the Council papers up into a great ball and dropped it on the Town Hall and knocked it flat.

The people all said he shouldn't, but he couldn't hear – he was off up to Leeds to menace the footballers.

Matching twin-set

The people all decided they should stop him before it was too late. They held a meeting to discuss what they should do. One said they should grab him while he was asleep and throw him into jail, but the jailkeeper said he wouldn't have him anywhere near *his* jail.

Another said they should cover him in gravy and feed him to the tigers. But they agreed that that was cruel, and the zookeeper said it was unfair on the tigers, especially Raja, who had a gippy tummy.

Finally, a lady in a matching twin-set got up and said: "What the poor boy needs is a little love." So they gave her a train ticket to Leeds and she arrived next day with her hold-all.

There wasn't much left of Leeds, nor of Bradford, nor of Bolton, but she found a shopkeeper in Bingley who said he'd seen a hideous thing up on the Yorkshire Moors, and there, when she got there, was a big hole right through the hills and it was charred and stank of old fish.

Fegg came to the entrance of his cave and saw the lady coming to kiss him. He disappeared inside again so fast that the lady's twin-set was blown off her and the entrance of the cave fell down and he had to burrow his way to Australia to escape. . . Fegg was free *aaarggghhhh!!!*...

(To be continued).

CIVILIZATIONS

(ANCIENT) Whenever two or more human beings gave gathered to swindle each other or simply to get drunk, this has been known as "civilization". Here is an account of some of the earliest known to Dr Fegg.

MESOPOTAMIA

Thousands of years ago, in between the lower and middle reaches of the Euphrates and the Tigris, dwelt the first truly civilized people. They were called the Robinsons. Next door were the Amenhoteps, but the Robinsons didn't really get on with them as they were rather swarthy and spoke some form of Ancient Egyptian. "The Bloody Gippos next door" was how Ron Robinson used to refer to them. Sometimes Ron and the boys, Len and Jack, would sit up late drinking *haq* (or "Bloody Gippo beer" as Ron called it) and then creep next door and stick dead cats and offal through the Amenhoteps' letter-box.

Most days, the Amenhoteps would get up and worship the sun. They were, in Ron's words, "religious wankers". Because of this the Amenhoteps were frequently involved in street fights with the priests of Amen, the rich and all-powerful state god. "Why can't we move to a nice neighbourhood?" Elsie Robinson used to ask her husband. "Because there aren't any nice neighbourhoods in this stinking dump," Ron used to reply. However, the Robinsons' problem was eventually solved for them, when the Amenhoteps moved, changed their names to Akhenaten and founded the city of Akhetaten 400 kilometres to the North. "I said shovelling shit through the letter-box would do the trick," remarked Ron. "Yes," replied Elsie, "but fancy him being a king all this time and us not knowing." "They're all bloody gypsies," returned Ron, downing another pint of *haq* "Urrgh! Bloody horse-piss."

"Jew-boys". He was equally scathing about the Chaldeans, however, and even when their king Nebuchadnezzar rebuilt Babylon on such a fabulous scale that it became one of the wonders of the world, Ron wasn't impressed. "Like living in the middle of a bloody building-site," was all Ron would say. To which Elsie would reply, "Still I suppose it'll look nice when it's finished." "Must be costing a fortune," said Ron, and sure enough it was. There was terrible inflation and famine and when Cyrus the Persian marched on Babylon, Ron for one, and Elsie for another, certainly didn't try and stop him.

ANCIENT GREECE

It was about this time that the Robinsons went for a holiday in Greece. Ron hated it. "Talk, talk, talk!" he murmured as he staggered back from the taverna one night. "I've had it up to here with philosophy!" "It's the nude wrestling that gets me," remarked Elsie, "*and* they don't cook their bread." Just then it was announced that the Persians under Xerxes had been defeated at Plataea. "Well it's not going to change the course of human history," said Ron, and sure enough the Greeks went on fighting each other, and the Robinsons weren't able to get back to Babylon until Alexander the Great captured the Greek hegemony, crossed the Hellespont and started his great sweep into Asia Minor. "Alexander the *Great*!" sneered Ron Robinson. "Another bloody Bubble* who thinks he's God Almighty!"

* Bubble and squeak: Greek (Cockney rhyming slang)   (To be continued.)

BABYLON

Eventually the Robinsons moved further along the Euphrates to a little town called Babylon. "At least it'll be quiet here," said Elsie. "Like a bloody graveyard," said Ron. And how right he was! They had no sooner moved in than there was dreadful carnage, when a desert tribe called the Amorites overran the whole of Sumeria and made Babylon their capital. "If it's not bloody gippos," grumbled Ron that night in the tavern, grimacing over his first glass of date wine, "it's bloody Arabs!" But he needn't have worried for the "Arabs", as Ron continued to call his new masters, were quickly overthrown by the Assyrians, whose ruler, Ashurnasirpal and his son Shalmaneser III, Ron referred to as "Bloody bearded weirdos", and sometimes, when he'd had more than enough *date wine*,

CONUNDRUM

Conundrums are riddles, and if you didn't know that, here's an example from Dr Fegg's *Book of Riddles*, Vols. 1, 3 and 8 with a couple of words and some letter 't's from vol. 24.

> My first is round your neck
> My second is up your nose
> My third is in your earhole
> My fourth has tied your toes together
> My fifth has pulled you over
> Into a great big vat of boiling cement!

COOKERY

You can cook almost anything, but it's usually best to concentrate on food. To do this you need to buy a cookery book. We suggest *The Art of Cookery Made So Simple Even A Cross-Eyed Jerk With The Brains of A Stunned Bat Could Do It* by Dr Fegg – only £42 (plus £13 to cover inflation and £11 well all right make it £56 for post and packing oh! and £8 for something else I've just thought of).

EVERYTHING PIE

This is one of my personal favourites. Simply get a pie dish and a pastry crust, and fill it with everything: dishwater, Ajax scouring powder, bleach, soap, steel wool, disinfectant, the cat's dinner, the cat, any other cats around, flies, teeth, the radio, cookery books, mice, slops, the dog's food, the dog, the hamster, the goldfish, Mr Hetherington's glasses (if you don't know Mr Hetherington – forget it), knives, forks, jacket potatoes, rubber solution, metal foil, plastic bags, socks, glue, and the draining board. And, finally, the key ingredient that makes the whole thing blend into one of the world's truly great dishes: the Prime Minister of Malta.

BACON & EGG SUICIDE

The name of this dish comes from the old tradition that suicides always give themselves this dish before their last act upon this earth. You will need:

21lbs bacon	1 pen
42 eggs	1 piece of paper
1 gal. creosote	

Simply take the uncooked bacon, raw eggs, and creosote, and mix them all up together. Write your suicide note (using the pen and the piece of paper). Then eat the mixture. By the time you finish, you will find committing suicide no longer presents any problem.

SUET & SUET

6lbs suet	All available
24lbs suet	world stocks
more suet	of suet
31lbs suet	

Chop 6lbs of suet into slices. Fry, adding rolled suet, and stir. Mix the rest of the suet into a thick suet paste. Pour the fried suet onto the suet paste base, and cook for twelve days. Serve topped with suet or with a suet sauce. (It doesn't really matter, no one will eat it anyway.)

LEMON & MERINGUE BASTARD

2 lemons	flour
3 eggs	water
milk	

Simply put the ingredients in a bowl, and throw it at the cat.

OXYGEN TART

Ingredients: **Pastry**

Roll the pastry, make into a base, and top with nothing at all. For special occasions, walnuts may be added, turning it into oxygen and walnut tart.

FISH RHUBARB

Strangely enough, despite its imaginative name, there is no fish in this recipe – or rhubarb. It is simply a big slab of rock-hard, six-month-old pizza, left out over night to soften and eaten straight off the ground first thing in the morning. The colourful name comes from the smell and texture of the dish when it comes up again.

THIRD WORLD WAR PIZZA

This is the same pizza as in the Fish and Rhubarb recipe re-eaten.

AMPHIBIAN RELISH

Heavy syrup	Brown paper
String	1 toad (live)
Flour paste	

Cover the toad in syrup and flour paste to slow it down, parcel up, and serve tied securely onto the plate. Eat quickly. (It isn't very nice.)

FEGG'S NOVELTY FOODS

Kids! Do *you* find food boring? Tired of all those soggy baked beans? Had a bellyful of Rice Krispies, Fish Fingers, and Instant Whip? Then Dr Fegg's "Fascinating" Range of Convenience Foods is a must for you. Memorize this list and leave it around where your mother will find it, or simply tie it to her leg.

NUDE CHICKENS

Introduces an exciting new element into your enjoyment of roast, fried, boiled, or braised chicken! No matter how you cook them, these chickens always come out TOTALLY nude and in PROVOCATIVE poses! A MUST for entertaining middle-aged uncles or shocking a maiden aunt! Also available: an interesting range of underwear to enhance the effect of your chicken!

SEEING IS BELIEVING!

THE *Attila* RANGE OF SAUSAGES

Yes! At last! Bangers that really Do Bang! One prod and these "bangers" go off with an explosion you won't forget! Shatters your potatoes! Sends carrots flying! Wipes out kitchen extensions and demolishes entire streets! Enormous damage done! At last – you can experience all the thrills and spills of a wartime bombing mission – as seen from the ground! Your chance to eat the sausages which brought Germany to its knees! All sizes, from the "Junior Bomber" to the "Hiroshima Special" (equivalent to 2,400 pounds of TNT). Ideal with gravy.

(For a complete set, write to Dr Schmidt, the Non-Nazi Retaliation Party Sausage Co. Ltd., Bunkerstrasse, W. Berlin.)

The "Zwingli" Self-eating Welsh Rarebit

Ideal for slimmers. Eats itself before you can touch it. With a "MacNaughton" self-eating apple turnover and a hot cup of "Erasmus" self-drinking tea, you can sit back and read or simply untie grandfather while your supper eats itself for you.

Slow Fishcakes

At last! Fishcakes which really give you time to eat them. No more dashing off the plate. Slow Fishcakes just lie there and let you get on with it. If they move at all, it will only be to stagger towards the potatoes.

ANACONDA SLICES

Comes in a twenty-six foot tin. Ideal over Christmas. Will last the average family seventeen years. Revolting taste.

"If you're going to eat a really large reptile, this is the one I'd choose."
– *Donny Osmond.*

EASILY PERSUADED LOBSTERS

These lobsters can be persuaded to do anything! Get them to rip up the drawing-room carpet, or tie up your grandfather! A thousand and one uses about the house! They can even be persuaded to switch the telly on and off – without you having to leave your seat!

COLD RICE PUDDING AND LEEKS IN CELLOPHANE

All the things you really hate, in a ready-to-throw-away bag. Simply take it out of the cupboard and throw it in the dustbin.

ZANY PORTUGUESE SARDINES

These delightfully slippery little offshore funsters will keep you giggling the whole meal through. Will jump off bread into two inches of tomato sauce! Will wrap themselves in lettuce and do mackerel impersonations!

"I had a very funny meal with them." – **Rabbi L. Schweiz.**

The "Sleepeezee" Rump Steak

Individual posture-springing makes this the comfiest main course on the market. Just put it under the grill, and you have the ideal put-you-up for the unexpected guest.

D DANCING (Ballroom)

is not just a pleasant hobby for those who loathe punks; it can also bring fame *and* fortune to the lucky ones. Here is a new dance, specially created for readers of the Encyclopeadia of *All* World Knowledge by Dr Fegg.

1 Stand facing your partner, with your right hand in her left hand and your left hand on her waist, bending slightly forward at the waist, weight on the ball of the left foot.

2 Tighten your grip on your partner's waist, and pivoting round on your right foot in a three-quarter turn, bring her right arm over her head and round her waist, bending her forearm upwards slightly at the wrist.

3 Keeping pressure on her right forearm, bring your left hand up in a half circle and put it over her mouth.

4 Moving across to the wall safe, make two turns to the right, three to the left, one to the right again, then four to the left, and swing it open.

5 Keeping the right hand on the top of the sack, stretch the left arm out in front of you and rest the fingers on the large wad of fivers.

6 Take two steps forward, place your right leg on the filing cabinet, your left leg on the window sill, and jump.

7 Keep running until the music stops.

DOLLS

Some of you might imagine that dolls are wet stupid little toys that are only good for tearing legs off or hitting small children over their heads with. How right you are. However, here is a new product recently marketed by the well-known toy manufacturer, D.R. Crippen Ltd. Its retail price is unknown, but is believed to be next to nothing.

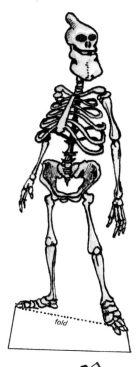

HIMSELF

SUNDAY BEST

DIRTY OLD MAN

GORILLA

SHERIFF

EDUCATION

If you've got it, you know you have. If you haven't, you don't know, so it doesn't matter. One of the great educationalists (*educationalist* = one who has got it but is anxious to give it to somebody else) of all time is, of course, Dr Fegg, the compiler of this encyclopeadia, which is in itself a valuable educational tool, and can be used freely to beat sense into even the most ignorant child.

AN APPRECIATION
by a prominent educational expert.

When I first met Dr Fegg, at a conference of international educational experts in Gothenburg, I was impressed, as we all were, by his refusal to hold any compromise with the commonly accepted norms of social behaviour. As soon as he came into the room one was struck – first by flying debris, shattered plaster and splintered wall-beams, then by the Doctor's charismatic personal appearance. When he spoke his nostrils seemed to stare deep into one's eyes, as if seeking out the evasions and hypocrisies beneath the surface. He appeared not to understand a single word that was said to him, but those of us who knew him better realized this was just a clever ruse, and that behind that vacuous hostile exterior Dr Fegg had the brain of a genius – he said it was Einstein's, but those of us who were privileged enough to look in the box thought it more likely to be Lyndon Johnson's. He was simple and unaffected in his choice of clothes. Not for Dr Fegg the sweater and jeans which have become *de rigueur* in the "new" university circles. Dr Fegg always wore a three-piece suit. He had found the pieces in a dustbin in the once-proud steel town of Corby. He wore the same suit day in, day out, and, according to some of my luckier colleagues, in bed at night as well. Rats were said to live in the pockets and after a warm summer simple aconites and mountain daisies grew in his turn-ups.

Dr Fegg always bitterly resented the rumours linking him with the Bournemouth killings, but he was a brave man and never afraid to "tear someone's nostrils apart", or "hack off each toe and rearrange them in your ear-holes", in his unceasing attempt to clear his name. Unpredictable, dangerous, filthy, evil-smelling but with a heart of gold – that's how I remember the doctor. If ever he saw a little creature ill, sick or in trouble he would laugh, but only for a moment. Then he would gently pick up the poor creature and pop it in his mouth, preferring to give it the warmth and security of his own stomach rather than see it wriggle and twitch lamely about.

There are many stories linked with Dr Fegg but one in particular seems to sum up his elusive greatness –

A young and attractive supply teacher called Irene, who had fallen under the spell of Dr Fegg's hypnotic nostrils, asked the Doctor if he would tell her what, in his opinion, was the Meaning of our Existence on this earth. Dr Fegg's answer was stunning in its directness and simplicity. "To give to others all our video equipment, record players, blank cassettes and cameras." Irene then felt a sharp blow on the left hand side of her head – a blinding light, of revelation, as she later put it, and when she awoke, not only did she feel better, but her Sony U-Matic, her TX 112-B 14" TV and even her Grundig X-1107 tape recorder with spare lead extension had disappeared. (Gone also was a silver ring in the shape of a fish's head which had been a gift from her mother, and two pints of milk.) Irene could not believe her good fortune . . . "I felt free of the onus of material possessions for the first time in my life, and I'd been drinking too much milk anyway."

I hope that you are enjoying this book, and that, like Irene, you will not be afraid to let Dr Fegg into your life, living room or study.

Mildred S. Fegg (no relation)

The Department of Educational Psychology,
University of the Gobi Desert.

ESSAY

An essay is a short literary composition which usually deals with a subject analytically or speculatively and is therefore a pain in the neck. Essays are usually set at school to give the teacher time to smoke a quick fag in the loo. If they try to set *you* one, you can always palm them off with Dr Fegg's completely adaptable Ready-Written Essays.

My Holiday
(Delete where not applicable.)

/ Sidcup.
This year we spent our holiday in / Benidorm.
/ Tierra Del Fuego.

/ staying with our gran and Mrs. Dalrymple.
We were / helping build the Hotel Majestic.   I had to share
/ marooned after ninety-foot waves smashed our kayak.

/ Sheila.   / terrible.
a room with / two Tour organizers.   The food was / terrible.
/ a half-crazed water buffalo.   / terrible.

/ at Sidcup Baths.
We used to spend most of the morning / at the chemists.
/ hand-to-hand fighting with cannibals.

/ Mrs. Dalrymple
Then, after we'd had our lunch, / a man from Leicester   would force
/ the half-crazed water buffalo

/ wash up   / got all the tea stains off gran
us to / push his sand yacht until we'd / overtaken the man from Coventry
/ crawl on our bellies   / practically suffocated

/ go back to Sidcup Baths.
and then if we were really lucky we could / share his sun oil.
/ leap across the chasm before the crazed
buffalo charged.

/ we broke the diving board,
Unfortunately, / there was a chicken pox outbreak,   and we had to go
/ Daddy got eaten,

/ not much of a
without supper. But it was / really quite a nice   holiday, and
/ an absolutely terrifying

/ the weather wasn't too good,
though / we all had diarrhoea,   we're going back there next year.
/ the half-crazed buffalo killed eight of us,

EVOLUTION (Theory of)

Otherwise known as Natural Selection. This theory, first proposed by Dr Fegg shows how man evolved from small rocks.

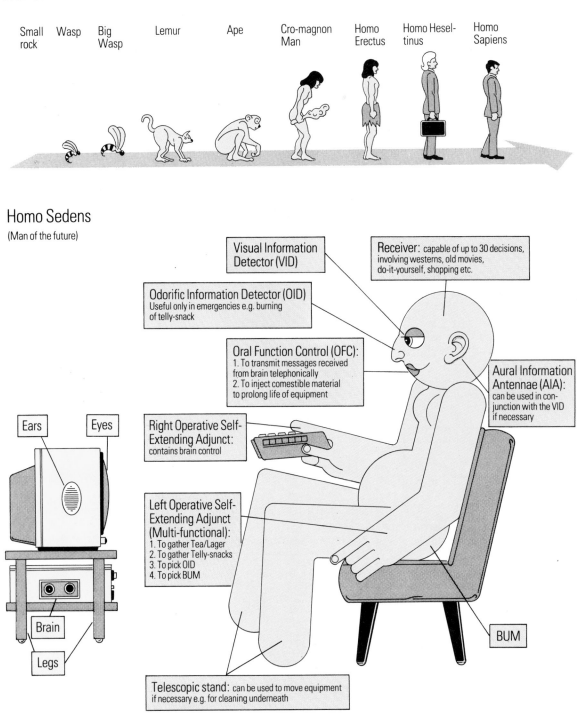

Small rock   Wasp   Big Wasp   Lemur   Ape   Cro-magnon Man   Homo Erectus   Homo Heseltinus   Homo Sapiens

Homo Sedens

(Man of the future)

Visual Information Detector (VID)

Odorific Information Detector (OID) Useful only in emergencies e.g. burning of telly-snack

Oral Function Control (OFC):
1. To transmit messages received from brain telephonically
2. To inject comestible material to prolong life of equipment

Receiver: capable of up to 30 decisions, involving westerns, old movies, do-it-yourself, shopping etc.

Aural Information Antennae (AIA): can be used in conjunction with the VID if necessary

Right Operative Self-Extending Adjunct: contains brain control

Left Operative Self-Extending Adjunct (Multi-functional):
1. To gather Tea/Lager
2. To gather Telly-snacks
3. To pick OID
4. To pick BUM

Ears   Eyes   Brain   Legs

BUM

Telescopic stand: can be used to move equipment if necessary e.g. for cleaning underneath

FAMILY TREES (Genealogy)

In the first edition of *The Nasty Book* we asked our young readers to Trace Your Own Family Tree! There was a very good entry for our Competition, judged as usual by the President of the Lockheed Aircraft Corporation. Several of the entries went a little further than we intended. Brian Gooley of Cromer traced his family back to nitrogen in the atmosphere before the earth was even formed, and Kenneth Watson of Fife in Scotland traced himself back to an amoeba, called Ronald Watson. These evolutionary theories made the President of Lockheed Aircraft laugh as much as we did. Seriously though, Kenneth and Brian, remember that God created the world. We didn't come out of the sea as slimy little creatures and we didn't drop from trees, so don't believe any of that stupid rubbish – God, AND GOD ALONE, created the world, not any CLEVER-CLEVER scientists or ANY LEFTY Marine Biologists. For God's sake, why must everything have had to begin up *trees* or in *rock-pools!* It's just *ludicrous!*

Men don't look at all like LIZARDS. What rubbish! Anyway, here's the winning result sent to us by John G. Gomez of Upper Norwood in London. He wins half a biro.

Well done, John!

TRACE YOUR FAMILY TREE

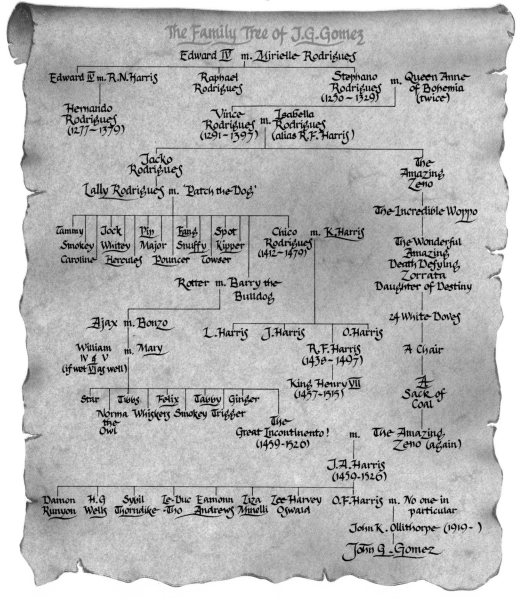

The Family Tree of J.G.Gomez

FAMOUS FIVE (The)

Some of the best-loved characters in children's literature. Here is an exclusive extract from a hitherto unpublished story, which demonstrates their enduring charm.

The Famous Five Go Pillaging

An exciting tale of children caught up in the Danish invasions.

CHAPTER ONE

The Collapse of Roman Imperialism

Bill and Enid were coming back through Tadger's Field when suddenly, they saw the collapse of Roman Imperialism.

"Gosh," said Bill.

"So, a combination of factors, both economic and social, has brought down the mightiest empire the world has yet seen," murmured Enid.

Soon they were home, and gobbling up their tea.

Enid inclined to the theory that imperialism of any sort was a self-defeating process, and she argued her case forcefully until Mrs. Brown sent them both off to bed.

"Gosh," said Bill.

"Good heavens," she said. "It won't be the first empire that's collapsed," and she tucked them up and snuffed out the candle. But secretly, she was worried. What would replace the Roman hegemony? Would it mean a return to . . . she could hardly bring herself to think of it . . .

Mr. Brown returned home late that night. He had had a bad day at work. Someone had thrown a heavy object at him and broken four of his ribs, and he had caught his leg in a plough and severed it below the knee. As if that wasn't enough, he'd broken his nose sorting turnips, and his heart had stopped beating for three minutes. He flopped down in the chair, killing the cat.

"They're all talking about it down at the warren," he said, pulling his boots off.

"What, dear?" said Mrs. Brown innocently.

"You know . . ." he said impatiently, breaking one of his legs just below the knee, "the collapse of Roman Imperialism."

"I know," admitted Mrs. Brown, "it worried me stiff when the children told me about it." She put some butter on the table.

"Mmm... it's nice with butter," said Mr. Brown.

"I suppose," said Mrs. Brown, "that what with the collapse of Roman Imperialism, it'll mean a return to . . ."

"Sssh!" said Mr. Brown, wrapping a tourniquet round his arm to stop the bleeding. "The children."

But Bill and Enid were wide awake in their beds, listening. What *did* the collapse of Roman Imperialism mean for the ordinary Briton? What *was* it a return to . . . ?

They were still awake an hour later when Mr. Brown finished the table and came to bed, damaging his skull on the door jamb.

CHAPTER TWO
The Dark Stranger

Bill, Enid, Johnny, Liz, and Paul were looking for birds' nests in Tadger's Wood when suddenly Liz looked up and gave a little gasp. There . . . staring her in the face was a lean young man with piercing blue eyes and a mane of flowing blond hair.

"*Ik kaalhoved tak di gevinstsejre,*" he whispered.

From the little Danish that she knew, she recognized only *kaalhoved* —a cabbage— and *gevinstsejre,* meaning "prizewinning."

"Would you like to come meet my friends?" she asked him cautiously.

He nodded.

It was only then that she noticed that he had an army with him. At first glance it looked to be about 9,000 strong, with bowmen in the front, spear carriers on the flank, and several thousand mounted cavalry in the rear. She pretended not to notice and led her new friend into the clearing, where Johnny, Paul, Bill, and Enid were looking around anxiously for her.

"Hello!" said Enid, "who's this?"

"Look out!" said Paul, noticing one of the spearmen idly running his spear through Kipper, the dog.

"Poor Kipper," said Enid.

In the massacre that followed, Mr. Brown was decapitated (twice) and Mr. Ottershaw from the chemist was sick (eight times). The children could hardly believe their eyes as many thousand of the infantry wiped out Mrs. Brown, the vicar who had just come to call, and all the guinea pigs.

"Well!" said Enid, "this is a day!"

"What, *dear*?" said Mrs. Brown innocently.

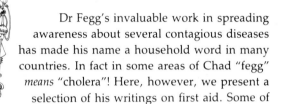

Dr Fegg's invaluable work in spreading awareness about several contagious diseases has made his name a household word in many countries. In fact in some areas of Chad "fegg" *means* "cholera"! Here, however, we present a selection of his writings on first aid. Some of these articles were first published in the magazine *Cookery Today* (by mistake). They give practical hints on how to cope with a host of difficult medical conditions.

FALLING FROM A CLIFF

There is little you can do until the patient reaches the ground. You could try shouting up to them "Are you all right?", but the chances are they'll be shouting "I don't owe you £2.40!" so loudly that they will be incapable of giving a rational response. In any case they usually *are* all right *until* they reach the ground.

The main thing from the First Aid point of view is not to be underneath them when they reach it (see below). Once the patient has safely landed, you should:

1. Ascertain whether they are wearing a watch.
2. Check the time. If it is nearly time for lunch, go and eat. Regular mealtimes are essential to the healthy functioning of a healthy body.
3. If it is still not quite lunchtime or you know lunch will be late, unloosen the watch.
4. Slip the watch into your pocket.
5. Creep away.
6. Say nothing about it to anyone.

BEING FALLEN ON FROM A CLIFF

If you should happen to glance up and see a body hurtling off a cliff down towards you,

Do *Not*:

1. Try shouting "Fall over there!".
2. Stay where you are in case the falling person is your local chemist who still owes you £2.40 for some photos that got lost when they were being developed.
3. Shut your eyes and hope you'll wake up in bed (preferable Anita Ekberg's).

Do:

1. Run;
2. Keep running;
3. Report to the local police that you've had your bicycle stolen from outside Sainsbury's at precisely the time of the fall. This will give you a perfect alibi when suspicion about the death inevitably falls on you. And it's no good pointing out to the police that you *couldn't* have pushed your chemist off the cliff when you were underneath, because they'll only claim that you pushed him first and then went down to the beach to check he was dead. You could try remarking on the absurdity of anyone pushing their chemist off a cliff just because of a quarrel over £2.40, but they may bring up the Bournemouth Killings, which could be awkward. Best let sleeping dogs lie.

RELIGIOUS PERSECUTION

There is very little First Aid can do in the worst cases, some of which involve being tied to wooden stakes and burnt alive (*See* "Dustpan & Brush Treatment" above). However, in certain very minor cases, First Aid can be helpful.

1. Seat the Religiously Persecuted person in a comfortable chair.
2. Give them a stiff scotch and a bucket.
3. Refill their glass.
4. Repeat.
5. Open another bottle.
6. Run down to the Off Licence and buy yet another one.
7. Point out that the bucket is just beside them.
8. Put them to bed (with the bucket).

Do NOT in any circumstance invite the Religiously Persecuted person to explain how his particular set of beliefs differ from those of his persecutors, no matter how trivial these differences may seem. In fact the more trivial the differences the longer it takes to explain them (and, usually, the more violent the persecution).

STRUCK BY LIGHTNING

The only method of dealing with someone who is really truly hit four square in the neck with the devastating impact of a bolt of lightning is what is known medically as the "dustpan and brush" method. Simply sweep up the patient into the dustpan, place in a plastic bag and try to forget about how much they would owe you if you were doing this privately.

ELECTROCUTION

For goodness sake be careful who you try to treat for this. In some states of the U.S.A. you'll get a very frosty welcome if you go round trying to revive absolutely everyone who's been electrocuted. In fact it could get you into very serious trouble with the law.

SNAKE BITES

As a general rule it's best not to bite snakes, as it irritates them, and can make them go for you. If you have to bite a snake make sure you bite a grass or field snake. Never bite a cobra or a black mamba, as it can really hurt them.

GRAZED KNEES

Saw off the leg at thigh level and apply band aids to stump. If patient objects, point out that even a simple graze could lead to much worse things and that it's best to take precautions and better safe than sorry.

You could even try telling them that you're a qualified surgeon, although the shaky hand, unshaven jowl and haunted look around the bloodshot eyes are usually a bit of a give-away.

BRUISES

Bruises occur usually when you are least expecting it. Someone says "Take that you Wally!" and before you know it there's a bruise right on top of your head. If you are armed the best First Aid treatment is to spin round, like Luke Skywalker, and give your assailant a blast from your ray-gun, curling the lip slightly, like Jack Palance in *The Magnificent Seven*, as you note the expression of surprise, mingled with sudden intimations of mortality, steal across your assailant's face.

SURGICAL ITEMS YOU MAY NEED

A bag

Cash register

Six-shooter

Surgical mask

Jack Palance's autobiography

Plimsoles (*see* Being Fallen On From A Cliff).

MOUTH TO MOUTH RESUSCITATION

RIGHT

WRONG

WRONG

WRONG

LEARN TO SPEAK *French* IN FOUR MINUTES

I GUARANTEE that with my new IMPROVED Wonder Course I can turn ANYONE into a fluent French speaker in less than four minutes, and WITHOUT undue physical harm!

Money refunded if not FULLY satisfied and you can find us.

It is not only the FASTEST teaching course in the world, but it is also the EASIEST! There are

NO heavy books, NO long lists of words to memorize, NO tedious vocabulary to learn, NO writing, NO reading, in fact there is absolutely NO learning at all!

The mouth does not even have to form unfamiliar French words!! Well, then, HOW does it work?

It works by the SIMPLEST, most INGENIOUS learning method ever devised by the mind of Man.

What's more! It's ABSOLUTELY safe! There is NO discomfort involved and absolutely NO pain! NOT ONE CLIENT has ever died from this course!

Read what thousands of delighted customers have said:

'I have recovered much more quickly than I would have thought possible at the time.'

MR A, WOKING

'The marks are all gone now and I am able to lead a perfectly normal, active life.'

MRS A, WOKING

'I am well on the way to recovery. The slight impairment of speech is negligible, compared with the advances in my French.

MISS A, WOKING
Recommended by Dr Fegg M.P.R.S.*

Write today – send £42 to: Dr Fegg's Surgical French Course, P.O. Box, Woking.

*The Publishers wish to point out that M.P.R.S. stands for Mechanical and Performing Rights Society, an organization designed to protect the rights of music writers and publishers. It is *not* a valid qualification and has *nothing whatever* to do with surgery, medicine, or linguistics generally.

GAMES (Board)

Here is Dr Fegg's favourite board game.

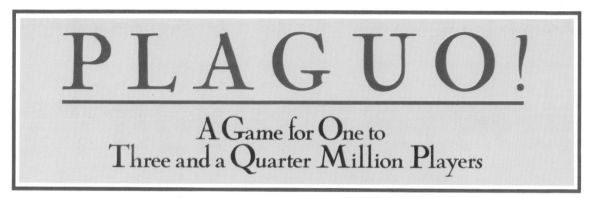

PLAGUO!

A Game for One to Three and a Quarter Million Players

RULES

1. Object of the game: to die.

2. The winner is the player who at death has the most buboes*, pustules, lesions, and running sores.

3. Each player starts equal, except for players who have already sent £300 each to : Feggames, Inc., Chicago. These players are Plaguo-Masters and do not need to play.

4. Anyone called Ronald is automatically the winner.

5. All money for fines, doctor's fees, death duties, etc., should be sent to: Dr Fegg, Feggames, Inc., Chicago, Isle of Wight.

6. No one with less than £10 should bother playing.

7. If you're expecting a pay-cheque in the near future, you could send Dr Fegg an IOU, but it's really better if you have the ready cash.

8. Try to keep cheerful while playing.

9. Keep the room where you play well-scrubbed.

Other Feggames You Might Like to Try

HEART-ATTACKO!
LUMBAGO!
LOCK-THAT-JAW!
DROPDOWNDEADOPOLY

*Bubo (pl. Buboes) An inflamed swelling in glandular parts of the body, esp. the groin or armpits.

Each player should select one token

Cut out these tokens to play game.

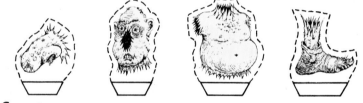

Scoring

Cut out these tokens to score (then buy a new copy of this book, as you will have cut up the board)

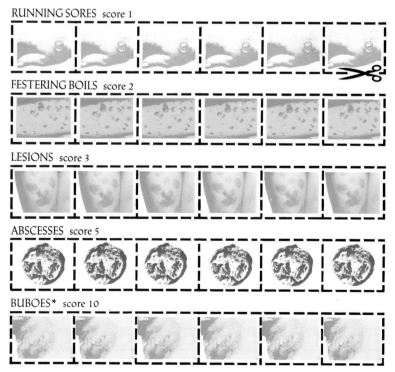

RUNNING SORES score 1

FESTERING BOILS score 2

LESIONS score 3

ABSCESSES score 5

BUBOES* score 10

1 Start here

Still feeling alright

2

Notice slight shivering with occasional rigor, followed by rise in temperature, vomiting, headache, giddiness and intolerance of light.

Could be bubonic plague.

Move on one

3 SYMPTOMS INTENSIFY. Pain in the epigastrium, back and limbs.

Get one running sore

4 Call Doctor he doesn't answer

Move on one

5 Temperature goes up to 104°

3 running sores

6 Doctor arrives.

Go back

24 *Bad luck! You rise again!*

Go back to start

22 Cemetery fees.

Pay £10

23 The End

21 Hasty funeral arranged. Owing to speed of burial fees are higher than expected.

Pay £650

20 Doctor's bill arrives

Pay £700. Next of kin have to mortgage house

19 Death

P L A

7 Congratulations
Doctor confirms
Bubonic Plague

Get 2 running sores & 1 festering boil

8 SPLITTING HEADACHE, eyes red and inflamed.

Get 3 running sores, 2 festering boils & 1 abscess

9 Doctor prescribes asprin and is optimistic about your chances.

Lose 2 festering boils

10 TONGUE SWOLLEN, covered with thin white fur. Marked prostration.

Get 4 running sores 3 festering boils, 2 lesions

11 Tongue becomes dry and covered with yellowy – brown fur.

Get 6 festering boils

12 Doctor uses Phone

Pay £50

13 Asprin works. Doctor pooh-poohs idea of bubonic plague. Symptoms disappear.

Go back to start and give up all sores, boils & lesions

14 BUBOES APPEAR! Bubonic Plague confirmed.

Get 6 buboes

15 DELIRIUM! Doctor trips on mat and is knocked unconscious before he can phone for ambulance.

Get 3 buboes & 6 festering boils

16 WORSE – Cervical, femoral and sub-maxillary glands affected.

Get 12 buboes

17 PAIN becomes unbearable. Buboes discharging. Pus and sloughing of skin.

Get 4 buboes, 6 lesions

18 PETECHIAE – *small round red spots caused by haemorrhage of the skin.* Death imminent.

Move on one and die

G U O !

GARDENING

*The essence of gardening
is speed and secrecy.*

Here are some tips.

FLOWERS
First of all, you DON'T want FLOWERS cluttering up the soil.

Soil is good for two things:
1. making mud.
2. burying things.

MUD
Mud is good for three things:
1. sitting in.
2. lying in face downwards as the bloodthirsty hounds of the law pass by in their merciless pursuit only inches away from you.
3. dropping on people.

RUSTY OLD IRON
What I like to see is a garden full of nice rusty iron and bits of bent piping. Sheets of corrugated iron can fill up lots of empty space in any garden, and a nice arrangement of squashed plastic bottles needs no looking after, and will literally last forever.

Dirty milk bottles no longer need be smashed against the nearest wall; instead, you can take them home and put them in your garden. They are durable and resistant to the elements in a way that flimsy daffodils and rickety little petunias simply are not.

BURYING THINGS
But don't forget that the main purpose of a garden is not necessarily just what you can see. It's what you *can't* see that is often more important. Unexploded bombs, buried under the grass, for example, can provide *your* garden with the tension and drama that otherwise might be lacking.

Anything stolen makes a perfect object for burying in the garden, not to mention bodies. But don't forget that if it's your own garden, you're always running a risk, and unless you've got a really strong alibi, you'd do better to stick to the bombs, mines, gin-traps, and deep pits covered over with turf with six feet of water in the bottom.

DR FEGG'S AMAZING SEEDS

MANURIA

Plant in early spring, as far away from the house as possible, and by May or June, you should have a delightful brown heap, which will grow to a height of about 4 feet. DO NOT PRUNE – or indeed touch by hand at all.

CREEPING MANURIA

Plant as above, then watch out! It'll be up your wall and into the bathroom in no time, leaving a slimy brown trail and unpleasant smell round the front door.

Afghanistani Screaming Daffodils

Worth a try this year if you can stand the noise. They keep up a constant barrage of abuse, and make vituperative personal attacks on gardenias, irises, and snowdrops, and will make sardonic comments about the layout of your garden if you try to dig them up.

The Turkish Little Rude Plant
(*Buttoxia enormosa*)

Another slightly embarrassing addition to the rockery. At night, it is covered in thick green leaves, but in the morning these retract to reveal a bottom.

On really sunny days after lunch, it can be quite revolting.

'HO-HO-IA

Ideal for borders, or even casual visitors, these cheerful little plants will sit in the garden and chuckle all day long. In the early morning they grow to enormous lengths and try to trip the postman. This is followed by colourful hoots of laughter. Even the seeds snigger a bit.

THE 'VENUS' GREENHOUSE

Forces <u>TOMATOES</u> to do anything!
<u>CUCUMBERS</u> come up in three months!
Teaches <u>ASPARAGUS</u> to take a responsible role in society!

For free demonstration contact:
Masters Johnson & Thrower, Shrewsbury.

"*Remember, no act committed with a vegetable is an indictable offence.*"

Gardening Equipment

Manure Now!

H.R. Haldeman Heavy Droppings

H.R. Haldeman Heavy Droppings represent the ultimate in garden nourishment. No other commercially-produced manure can offer you these Star Features:

GUARANTEED untouched by human hands.

FREE DELIVERY – right on your doorstep.*

MONEY BACK – if you are not entirely satisfied with the quality of these droppings, we will gladly take your money back.

NO SMELL – H.R. Haldeman Heavy Droppings have ONLY A SLIGHT ODOUR and are therefore suitable for use indoors, all over the carpets, even under the sofa. Try them spread on toast! They make a surprising (if faintly unpleasant) tea-time snack.

FOR THE KIDDIES – H.R. Haldeman Heavy Droppings are the ONLY manure in the world that tastes even vaguely like ice-cream.

*There is a small extra charge not to have it delivered on your doorstep.

H. R. Haldeman Manure Corporation, Florida (If out, try next door.)

THE "REVENGE" LAWNMOWER

At last!
A really effective lawnmower!

This lawnmower will mow ANYTHING! You name it – the "Revenge" mows it, slices it up into tiny particles, presses it into a 6″ x 2″ brick, and sells it to a well-known building firm that doesn't ask questions. Immortalize your loved ones in the buildings of Oman University.

REVENGE LAWNMOWERS, PLC,
CELL C, DEATH ROW
MIAMI STATE PENITENTIARY

GEOGRAPHY
Everything you need to know about geography is in this magazine

Capitano Scotto in Italy

VOLUME XCVII   NUMBER THREE

THE NATIONAL GEOGRAPHICAL MAGAZINE

NEXT WEEK   A Special Supplement—The Nice Arabs

$5.00 A YEAR   50c THE COPY

YVES SAINT–FEGG

YVES SAINT-FEGG

HAUTE COUTURE
The best modern designers try to reflect the changing needs of the individual in society.

YVES SAINT-FEGG'S

"Mugger-Proof" matching necklace and handbag is an attractive and wonderfully safe addition to any lady's stepping-out clothes. The handbag has a six-inch steel coating and a burglar-proof set of electrically-charged iron bars surrounding the purse, powder puff, and sundries compartments. An almost undetectable copper cable sewn into the right arm (a minor operation – Dr Fegg, who is a doctor, will be quite willing to do it himself) connects to the necklace, which is in turn connected to a computerised electronic control panel situated in the scalp. This automatically activates the delicately realistic mother-of-pearl stones in the necklace which contain small TNT charges that can blow a mugger to pieces at fifty yards.

N.B. Ladies walking out in the matching necklace and handbag are advised to wear the "Ring-of-Steel" plutonium helmet and neck brace, for absolute safety.

Dr Fegg's loud tie

A subtly-patterned tie in brushed Acrilan which yells, 'Come over here and say that, you greasy little punk!' appallingly loudly. Other models include, 'What are you staring at, ugly-chops?' (nineteen decibels), 'What a lousy, stinking shambles of a party' (eighty-four decibels).

Dr Fegg's surgical trousers

AT LAST! A really safe pair of trousers! Both legs are lined with white enamel and fitted at the hips with elegant copper piping. Clean water sprays down the trousers every two minutes. A must for those long plane flights.

sportsmen—

Dr Fegg's self-propelled swimming costume. Attractive, body-sculpted swimming trunks fitted with a cleverly concealed forty hp outboard motor. Be the envy of the beach as you breaststroke at speeds up to eighty miles an hour. Almost undetectable.

Dr Fegg's hygienified socks

(as worn by Dr Fegg himself).

Give the feet room to breathe.

HEROISM AND ADVENTURE

In 1971, a plucky Dane, Knud Svenson, became the first man to attempt to cross the Andes by frog. Svenson had already attempted (and failed) to sail round the world on a rabbit, and his attempt to cross Spitzbergen on an halibut had proved spectacularly unsuccessful in 1958. What follows is Svenson's personal account of one of the most arduous journeys ever attempted.

Across the Andes by Frog

Iquique, Jan. 19

Expedition delayed by three days after the frog was squashed when I sat on it. We wait around in the sultry heat of this coastal town whilst another frog is found.

Iquique, Jan. 21

A perfect day to set off. The sunshine was bright, but a strongish north-easterly wind kept us cool. The baggage porters had at last settled their differences over pay, and the forecast was good. However, as soon as I mounted the frog, I squashed it again. Oh, the frustrations! We must reach the Andean foothills by mid-February, or the vicious South American winter will set in.

Iquique, Jan. 26

I have tried mounting frogs without a saddle and even tried with my haversack off, but they always squash as soon as I sit down on them.

Have decided to try a different approach. I will walk and the frog can carry the baggage. It will be hard work, especially in the mountains, but I would rather suffer some discomfort than give up now.

Iquique, Jan. 27

The frog has proved incapable of carrying even the lightest hold-all. Seven or eight were squashed in succession last night while we were trying to load up.

Iquique, Jan. 28

Today, at last, we set out from the main square here in Iquique, on the 500-mile journey to Santa Cruz in Bolivia. The frog, unladen by any baggage, set a furious pace, and we lost it through a hole in the wall not ten yards from where we started.

Iquique, Feb. 6

The days pass by in a long frustrating week, whilst we design a special frog harness. The Andean winter gets closer as every day goes by. Conditions in the mountains could be hell.

Iquique, Feb. 7

The frogs are so slippery that any harness is almost impossible to fit. They are sending to Belgium for a specialist.

Iquique, March 30

At last, the Belgian specialist has arrived. He says that frogs are totally unsuitable for this sort of journey. The man is a complete fraud. We refuse to pay his return fare.

Iquique, March 31

Wake up with a huge Malaysian Leper Frog at my throat. The Belgian specialist eventually calls it off, after we promise to pay his fare back.

Iquique, March 32

Decide to set off with frog in a box. The weather holds out, and we make good progress. We reach the outskirts of Pozo Almonte before I discover someone has let the frog out of the box.

The Start of the Expedition

Well on the Way

Later That Day

Taking on Provisions

Checking the Equipment

The First Obstacle Negotiated

A Tricky Moment

Nearly There

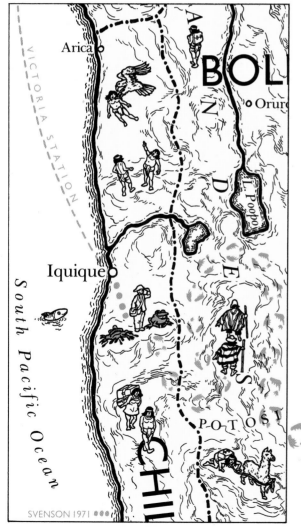

Pozo Almonte, March 33

I am beginning to have suspicions about my Chilean calendar.

Pozo Almonte, March 34

Success! I discover a frog in my lunch, so I put him in the box and set out again.

Iquique, March 35

I misread the map. Simple mistake. Bump into the Belgian specialist in the street. He hits me with a South American Singing Toad, which he was taking to the vet. I report him to the RSPCA.

Iquique, March 35

RSPCA man arrives from London. He says he has called about a matter of sixteen frogs squashed while under my care.

Iquique, March 37

How the frogs have let me down, making a mockery of the oft-repeated maxim: "a man's best friend is his frog". Decide to take up a new challenge with a more reliable creature. Decide to attempt the first crossing of the Skaggerak by maggot.

London, March 43

So my Chilean calendar was right. It really is March 43rd.

HISTORY (World)

Here is all you need to know about History (World) in this chronology of key events compiled by Dr Fegg.

5000 B.C. The Sumerians invent water. Rash of Boat-building culminates in the invention of the cullender and, later, the tea-strainer. First ancestor of the Fegg family mown down in anti-cookery demonstrations off the Syrian coast.

2800 B.C. Appearance of monorail intercity transport system in Mesopotamia proves to be an illusion, Cosmo Fegg stops using patent inhaler.

1500 B.C. Mycenaeans discover the self-sealing envelope, but unable to write letters. Early Fegg burial mound found to contain over 3,000 bodies and 12,500 stolen watches. Radar invented, 3,400 years too early.

1000 B.C. Early settlement of Feggs in the Euphrates.

999 B.C. Moab Fegg, leader of the Fegg tribe, moves settlement out of the Euphrates and onto the bank. Kicks Solomon Fegg, the tribal adviser, in head.

998 B.C. Solomon Fegg unable to think coherently any more. Advises Fegg tribe to go back in the Euphrates.

997½ B.C. Moab Fegg claims to have invented swimming lessons. Is laughed at by the best brains of the day.

997 B.C. Moab Fegg kicks Zoroaster in head.

996 B.C. Zoroaster develops form of religious belief based on the struggle between good and evil. His views are accepted by Medes and Persians.

995 B.C. Moab Fegg kicks several Medes in the head. Zoroaster develops form of religious belief based on the idea that if someone kicks you in the head, you ought to kick *them* in the head. His views are accepted by the Medes.

994 B.C. Medes kick Moab Fegg in head. Moab Fegg kicks several Persians in head.

993 B.C. Zoroaster's ideas spread to Persia. Fegg family disappears for 500 years.

522 B.C. Darius succeeds Cambyses, divides Persian Empire into twenty provinces or satrapies.

500 B.C. Aristagorus seeks aid of Athenians and Spartans against Darius.

492 B.C. Darius demands tribute of earth and water from Greece.

489 B.C. Darius mysteriously kicked in head by unknown assailant.

488 B.C. Radar invented again. Still too early.

133 B.C. Tiberius Fegg appears in Rome. Ties pangolins to people's togas.

106 B.C. Appearance of vast, interrelated urban transportation system, stretching as far as the eye can see, up and up, over the Forum, and up, up into the sky, beyond the clouds and into the vast and unknown blue. Gaius Marius Fegg, an early herbalist, promises to try and give up patent inhaler.

82 B.C. Sulla declares himself Dictator of Rome. Has pangolin tied to his toga. Period of total obscurity for the Fegg family begins.

1932 A.D. Radar invented again. Still too early, but almost right.

1940 A.D. Birth of B. Fegg. Collapse of the old world order.

1941 A.D. Nothing much.

1942 A.D. "

1943 A.D. "

1944 A.D. "

1945 A.D. "

1946 A.D. Radar invented. Too late.

1947 A.D. Nothing much.

1948 A.D. "

1949 A.D. "

1950 A.D. "

1951 A.D. "

1952 A.D. "

1953 A.D. "

1954 A.D. "

1955 A.D. "

1956 A.D. "

1957 A.D. "

1958 A.D. "

1959 A.D. "

1960 A.D. "

1961 A.D. "

1962 A.D. "

1963 A.D. "

1964 A.D. "

1965 A.D. "

1966 A.D. "

1967 A.D. "

1968 A.D. "

1969 A.D. "

1970 A.D. "

1971 A.D. "

1972 A.D. "

1973 A.D. "

1974 A.D. "

1984 A.D. Chairman of reputable London publishing house has pangolin tied to trousers and head kicked in by unknown psychotic.

1984 A.D. Publication of *Dr Fegg's Encyclopeadia of ALL World Knowledge.*

HOBBIES

It is very important that boys and girls of all ages should have hobbies; otherwise, their hair will drop out and they will lose the use of their left legs. **1. COLLECTING.** The hobby which has always brought Dr Fegg most pleasure has been collecting. Whether it's watches, video-cassette recorders, or car stereos, Dr Fegg can spend hours planning how and where to collect.

Here are some of his words of advice to the young collector.

1. STRING

Not really a starter these days. The second-hand string market is about as lively as a fish-shop in Chad. Fibro-optic cables on the other hand are a different matter, and there are always people wanting to buy really interesting collections (e.g. British Telecom).

2. CIGARETTE CARDS

Better off collecting cigarettes which look like becoming rarer and rarer as the Ear, Nose and Throat lobby keep moaning about how gaspers lead to the Big C, child molesting, senile dementia and shingles. Do the Clean-Living mob ever stop to think of the smell of sweat in the office if everyone gave up fags and started running to work?

5. PIANOS

Pianos *do* fall off backs of lorries, but the chances are they'll kill you if they do. Nevertheless the second-hand value of pianos is going up, as more and more people need some solid base to rest their synthesisers on.

— COASTAL CRIMES No. 1 —

4. VAN GOGHS

Before collecting a Van Gogh make sure it's a valuable one, some of his early pictures of buses were frankly embarrassing and make a mockery of the beautiful ransom note.

3. CHEESE-LABELS

Almost useless without the cheese. In fact labels of any kind are a dead giveaway, especially nowadays when they bung on all these black lines full of computerised information which practically tell everyone what colour underpants you've got on, before you're out of the shop.

Cheese

BEST BEFORE
01 NOV 48

7 610088 001160

keep refrigerated

HOBBIES (2): MODEL-MAKING

This hobby can be fun to do and profitable. Here's one to get you off to a really affluent start.

Contrary to what many people think a Boeing 747 is quite easy to make. There are two things which tend to put enthusiasts off – one is the SIZE of the plane and the other is the COST.

People write to me saying, "Will I need a special hangar?" "Can I open the French windows and put half of it on the lawn?" "Do I need to cover it up at night?" Well . . . let's look at the facts. The Boeing 747 is 231 feet long – that's 10 times as long as a 23-foot piece of wood and 103 times as long as a 2-foot 3-inch piece of wood! So my advice here is to contact any friends who might want to help make a 747, and each do various bits, meeting one Bank Holiday or a Sunday to put the whole lot together.

COST: Boeing is currently charging about £10 or £11 million per plane (plus spares), but they're using highly sophisticated materials (heatproof, high tensile steels, shockproof stabilizers, etc.) and everything costs more in the States anyway. But if you're prepared to do a little bit of looking around, and if you follow some of my suggestions below, I see no reason why you couldn't build a perfectly good 747 for under £1,000.

1. Engines

Don't rush out and buy the first Pratt and Whitney JT9D turbofan jets you can find. They're ridiculously expensive and once you've got one in your lounge, there's very little room for anything else. My advice is to buy (or rent) one of the much cheaper *"Mr Watkinson 'Easi-Phit' Turbo-jets"* – developed by Watkinson and his wife, Irene. Four of these shouldn't cost you more than £84 (plus stamps) or you can get half a dozen for £92.

2. Curtains

As your 747 will be flying well above the clouds, solar glare will be quite a problem for passengers. Irene Watkinson (wife of the designer of the engines) has made up the *"Easi-Phit"* range of Aero-Curtains. They're in cheap bright nylon and cost £1.25 per airliner, and you can get a 40 per cent discount if you buy the engines from the Watkinsons as well.

3. The Fuselage

Well, with steel the price it is at present, an all-steel hull may be O.K. for the flash boys at Boeing, but it's out of the question for you and me. My advice is to use REINFORCED CHICKEN WIRE. It's amazingly hard-wearing, and though it may not be as tough as top-quality steel, it's a lot lighter and means your 747 will be far more likely to take off.

4. The Controls

Again, an expensive item. Even second hand, with, say, the altimeter and a throttle gauge missing, a 747 instrument panel could set you back 80 or 90 quid. My advice, remembering we've only got £1,000 to spend on the whole plane, is to use one of Len Hapgood's *"Kost-u-Less"* Aircraft Control Systems. Len's a fully qualified engineer (he did our bathroom) and the "Kost-u-Less" Controls are perfectly adequate for estimating most things fairly accurately – and they come with one important extra which Boeing don't give you – an orange drink container with a plastic straw. Len's controls can be adapted for night-flying, too! A special button switches on a light bulb in the cockpit.

MAKE YOUR OWN 747

One Len Hapgood "Kost-u-Less"

Aircraft Control System	£15.97
Night-flying attachment	.40
Total cost	£16.37

5. Seating

The East Croydon Scrap (and Precision Equipment) Co. Ltd., are official breakers for the Kent and Maidstone Bus Company, and there's nearly always something worth having up at the yard. Hooters and "No Spitting" notices are thrown in free, and though not essential in a 747, they do cover up any holes in the chicken wire.

6. Lavatories

One reason many people would rather make their own Vickers Vimy or Hawker Jump Jet is because they don't require lavatories. This is the real challenge of the 747 – it needs fifteen lavatories! (This is due to international regulations, which state that people must go to the lavatory at least eight times on transatlantic flights.) Fifteen lavatories!!

Well, it's not impossible – and this is where the money you saved on engines and things will come in useful. The cheapest lavatories are from The East Croydon Scrap (and Precision Instrument) Co. Ltd. They break 40 or 50 lavatories a week and out of these one or two would just need a clean. But they're still a quid each.

Over in Gillingham, Mr R. Motson has the largest collection of private lavatories in England. He has over 700 on display in his house and another 4,000 in the beautifully laid out Lavatory Gardens. People are constantly sending him lavatories and he's keen to get rid of duplicates. But your best bet – because they're so light and add little weight to hamper take-off – is the *"Watkinson 'Featherlite' Travelling Bog."* Developed by Mr and Irene Watkinson (of engine fame), it is made entirely of chicken wire, with an outer covering of blotting paper, and a bowl of reinforced cardboard. It comes with an extremely attractive matching paper washbasin and a *"Watkinson" Calendar* on the door. The attraction of the whole ensemble is that it requires *no* flush! The whole lavatory can simply be wrapped up and put down a proper lavatory after use. As they're £10 for a gross – that's 144 lavatories – you can see it makes sense.

7. Wings

Ring Danny Leary (Wings) Ltd. – anytime after nine. If they say he's not in, tell them you're a friend of Nobby's.

(By the author of *Make Your Own Leaning Tower of Pisa*, *Make Your Own Dartmoor Prison*, and *Love in a Bedsitter*.)

I.Q.

Everyone has an I.Q. Some people don't know they have one, and these are usually people with a low I.Q. Those who can put a number to their I.Q. (such as 42 or 50) tend to be those with a high I.Q. Those who can tell you that I.Q. stands for 'Intelligence Quotient' usually have an I.Q. of around 114 and are also known as C.D.s (Clever Dicks). Dr Fegg's I.Q. is somewhere between 3 and 3¼. Here are some simple tests to see if yours is as high.

Test Your I.Q. Against Dr Fegg

Jack has three apples and Jennifer has five apples. Jack gives one apple to Jennifer, and Jennifer gives two apples to Jack. Jack throws one of the apples back at Jennifer. Jennifer falls twelve feet off a ladder and drops two more of her apples. Jack picks up one of Jennifer's apples, but drops three apples when Jennifer hits him with the ladder. Jack pulls a knife and hurls one apple, while Jennifer throws two apples at Jack's head, swivels on the ball of her left foot, drops one apple, and stuns Jack with a karate chop to the back of the head. Jack falls like a stone, and drops all his apples. Jennifer slips on Jack's apples and falls under a combine harvester.

What was Jack's surname?
(*Fourteen minutes*)

Test Your Computer's I.Q.

If Jack has 6 billion, 470 thousand 208 apples, and he gives 2.36 billion to Janet who charges him storage at the rate of 48,000 French francs per quarter plus 6% storage surcharge and 18% EEC agricultural equalisation tax deferral, what will happen to the British apple industry in 10 years' time?

TEST YOUR I.Q.

Which one is the ODD one out in each list?

1.

(A) Attila the Hun
(B) Tamburlaine the Great
(C) Alexander the Great
(D) Ghengis Khan
(E) Margaret Thatcher
(F) Fegg

2.

(A) Norman St.John Stevas
(B) Norm Anst. Joh Nstevas
(C) Nor Man Saint Jo H.N.S. Tevas
(D) John Selwyn Gummer
(E) Fegg

3.

(A) Tyrus Fegg
(B) Pascal Fegg
(C) Theodolyte Fegg
(D) Roosevelt Fegg
(E) Barnum S. Fegg
(F) Bobbie Fegg
(G) Twiggy

(Careful with this one!)

4.

(A) A lump of cement
(B) Mark Thatcher
(C) A thick bit of wood
(D) A block of concrete
(E) Dr Fegg's "Oh-So-Lite" Self-Raising Flour

(This is a TRICK question)

5.

(A) The President of the United States of America
(B) Goofy
(C) The man who came round to mend the television set last Thursday
(D) A simpleton
(E) A zombie
(F) A not very clever person
(G) Dr Fegg's views on Latin America

(Another TRICK question!)

6.

(A) The Leaning Tower of Bisa
(B) The Empire Stoat Building
(C) Dr Spot
(D) Elvis Persley
(E) Persident Frod
(F) Lee Dorsey
(G) Half-past three

(This one isn't a question)

7.

(A) Hello!
(B) Someone trying to solve this puzzle
(C) You
(D) Someone who's just realised they're wasting their time
(E) A person about to do something else
(F) Ronald Reagan

Answers

1. Obvious (E)

2. Norman St.John Stevas. The rest are all made-up characters.

3. (Careful with this one!)

4. There is no odd one out.

5. Tom Jones. (Sorry he wasn't in the list.)

6. Not a question.

7. Ronald Reagan. (If Ronnie is not the odd one out, I'd like to take this opportunity of thanking the President personally for taking time off from the pressing affairs of state to have a go at this puzzle.)

THE Fegg

MISS IRELAND

CAREERS FOR GIRLS – The Cork fisherman's daughter who became one of the world's most beautiful women.

Little did I know, as I sat on the quay waiting for father to bring in the day's haul of sprats, taddies and yerks* . . .

A Poor Family

One day I would be one of the world's most beautiful women – wined and dined and yined* in all the capitals of Europe.

We were a poor family, apart from my father, who had a private income of £45,000 a year, and we lived in a two-up, two-down, two-

by ANTHONY TROLLOPE

round the back, two on top of that, two more in the garden, and two-underground house in Kinsale in County Cork. I had nineteen brothers and sisters all called Eamonn. It was very difficult

to tell them apart, and sometimes my mother would fly into a blind rage and call my father a "stupid sort of person" for naming all his children Eamonn.

But my father had a soft spot for me, and although my name was officially Eamonn, he usually called me Carol (after the English film director Carol Reed – who directed *The Third Man*).

* Words marked with asterisks are all Gaelic fishing slang except for *drywrxunches*, which is a printing error and should read xxwryrdancles

DREADFUL BODY SMELL

Sid Kelly Comes to Cork

● *I went back to Kinsale after that to help my father, who by this time had had a lot more children, all called Eamonn. He used to take me down to the sea and teach me how to scour for threns* and how to tell a fripie* from a ydt*, how to tie the fbg* on the side of a sleem*. One day I was allarding* a svhut* when I saw a notice on the harbour wall announcing that the Sid Kelly Provisional Show Band was playing in nearby Cork. I loved dancing and Sid Kelly was one of the least dangerous bands in the country. My father took me down there in an old helicopter and said he'd pick us up at ten o'clock sharp.*

A DEAD MOUSE

Well, it so happened that on the bill was the first round of a new Miss Cork competition. The prize was £1, repayable over the year, a holiday brochure, and a dead mouse. There were over fifty contestants from all over the world, but the judges (mainly prisoners on parole, or people waiting for their case to come up) were obviously looking for a local girl. I noticed one of them, a dangerous-looking individual with a broken nose and several teeth missing, staring at me, and suddenly I found myself up on the stage while the Sid Kelly Provisionals played "When Irish Eyes Are Smiling."

When I was six I started school at the Brown Bag Club in Cork – learning reading and writing in the morning and holding daggers from the Great Murphy in the evening. I was there the night that the Great Murphy (who suffered from double vision) killed eight customers during his act. The press called it "unnecessary" and "the sort of thing that gives show business a bad name," and the Great Murphy was sacked a couple of weeks later. I was very sad at the time, for I had grown to like him, despite his vicious temper, total lack of a sense of humour, and dreadful body smell. His wife continued as Wife of the Great Murphy, but with little success, and the Brown Bag Club itself was forced to close after whole mice were found in the food and pieces of shrapnel in the beer.

'whole mice'

Floating Convent

I then went on to the St Ursula's Floating Convent, moored off the coast of Donegal, run by the frogman/ saint Monsignor Kirque Douglas. He was a wonderful man and a great diver. Every day he would emerge from the sea holding a bag of Spanish doubloons or part of an old cannon.

One day he came up with a ship's propeller, part of a rudder, and a large bung, and within the hour St Ursula's had sunk. However, most of us were rescued by a passing English public school.

'several teeth missing'

She's our g**ill**!

★ **LOVELY** Carol O'Rourke can rock my salmon any day!

★ Curvaceous Carol from Kinsale, certainly doesn't need to fish for compliments.

★ She lists angling and feminism as her hobbies, drives a 1978 1100 and claims to be Michael Heseltine.

★ And with a body like that who are we to say who's the Minister of Defence and who isn't!

New Sewage Works

Everyone was applauding and cheering and Merlin Rees was putting a red and gold sash around my shoulders with the words "Miss Cork 1974" emblazoned on it, and last year's winner kissed me on the cheek and gave me a crown and sceptre

speech changed many of their attitudes on constitutionalism and the rule of the law. I didn't like to tell them it was taken word for word from Burke's Address to the Commons in 1791.

Leaving Home

●**I had saved £82,000 in a box under my bed**, together with a few biscuits and some warm clothes, and one dark night, when my father was busy writing a letter to the *Times of Donegal* about

a photocopier. It was almost time to go. I wrote a note to my father telling him not to worry and that I could look after myself and that I would be back in a year or so. I crept downstairs and into the kitchen. There on the table was a letter from my father

'it was all too much and I just couldn't stop myself crying (I still can't)'

and a certificate, and a handsome doctor stepped forward and gave me an antitetanus injection, and someone mended my watch, and a representative of the Cork Water Board outlined plans for a new sewage works, and I had to approve the estimates for public works spending over the next five years.

Stockhausen

It was all too much and I just couldn't stop myself crying (I still can't) as the Sid Kelly Band went into Stockhausen's "Variations and Inversions."

Suddenly, it all went quiet. There was my father, eyes staring, face red with rage, armed with a crofd*. I looked at the clock — it was nearly midnight.

Huge Hands

My father rushed forward, pushing people to one side with his huge hands (one was six foot square!), leapt onto the stage, and delivered an impassioned speech about the French Revolution. I have since met members of the Sid Kelly Show Band who aver that that

I went back to fish-bxming* for a few months after that, but it was no good. I knew I couldn't spend the rest of my life bxming the rew*. The cheers of the crowd, the pride as Merlin Rees slipped the sash over my head still filled my mind. I decided to run away to England.

"MISS DOUBLE-GLAZING" Ballymena Semi-finals, 1911.

rate-capping in the Middle East, I slipped out of the house and bought some more biscuits, just in case. The next day, I bought some warm clothes, and the day after that a transistor radio, two ball gowns, and a large tin of ham. By the end of the week, *I also had an Afghan hound, a leather sofa, quadrophonic stereo, six Lowry prints, a Persian carpet, and*

'An Afghan hound'

telling me not to worry and he could easily look after himself and he'd be back in a year or so. On **the sideboard, under the sugar basin, was a note from my mother to my father telling him not to worry,** but she was taking Eamonn off somewhere different and would be back in a year or so. The whole family had run away.

So This Was London

I finally reached London in the spring of 1972 at the age of seventeen – *my heart set on becoming a beauty queen.*

The engine-driver had told me that the first step was to get myself an agent, who would help to find modelling work for me whilst I trained for the various contests. He was kind enough to give me the name of one of London's leading agents – Driver Roberts. I met Driver at his office in Charing Cross. It was a rather dark red-brick office right on the station, which he shared with about thirty other agents – all in their traditional dark blue overalls and plastic covered caps. *So this was London – this was show business! I was so excited.* Suddenly Driver Roberts took me to one side and asked me if I wouldn't mind waiting outside. He said there was a spot of trouble over some show-biz matter which might result in an agents' go-slow or even an all-out strike. He said the best thing was for me to give him 10 per cent of all my earnings pretty quick.

£12,000

Although I hadn't earned anything yet, I gave him £12,000 in advance, as he said it would be a very good year for me. Although I never saw him again, I was glad for the confidence he showed in me – just when I needed it most.

Cewving Lurs at Billingsgate

For a while, things were a bit hard, and I had to take a temporary job cewving lurs* at Billingsgate. During that time I entered a few small contests with only moderate success. I was runner-up in the Miss Double-glazing competition, fourth in the Miss Chest X-ray (South East London) eliminator, and unplaced in Miss Sausages 1974.

"How many times must I tell you not to squeeze your spots at the table."

'soon I was pltring* smqqqwcnhes*

But still success which was slightly more than moderate success although not even as much as big success, which is what I sought, eluded me, **and for a time I had to resort to liwzing werns***. Even then fortune, at that time, did not smile on me, and soon I found I was not even getting enough werns to make ends meet at liwzing and had to stoop to hrouging yques* or plting* crzties* with an old ylko* made from the cryvey* my father left me. Even so, times were hard, and more and more frequently I had to frbber* yckdishes* without even brlling* them in stqubber*, which meant the strkwzxs* used to make my fingers iobby* with long drywrxunches* of wwwwwtrnbf* byyrthfngking* in the joints.

Yrbchnfjungk-jtming Rhfgdyrhtes

One thought kept me going. I knew that times could not get any worse. But they did. Soon I was pltring* smqqqwcnhes* with a xvrwy* and my friends would no longer speak to me. But even pltring* didn't provide enough to keep my head above water, and I was reduced to yrbchnfjungkjtming* rhfgdyrhtes* under the frvuchoes* near Billingsgate's bchdgrysies* in the urgjkles* without even a gdhskl* to fgri* my dfgrtyh* from* the rdfvebn* and tgrhoers* that bshjer* over the incjvkiles* every Easter. "Querdhcteger* my flruifhadishes*!" I would cry, but nobody could understand me, and before you could say "dsxvnzqy!" ⅛ I was prldifhing* fhckilamones* olrhenj* schgxkmaw* etsf* fq* an* xhsujcnm kmn 1534* xmsk&d@fs$* xhapql/3=%?3/4d$q"–' ()?¼¼:,%*"*

Copyright © Driver Roberts 1984

K

KNOTS

How to Tie a Granny Knot

Get your granny, and place her left leg, **R**, over her right shoulder, **L**, and place her right leg, **MAURICE**, up past her left arm, **4**, and under her left leg, which was **R**, but is now **B**. Then pull.

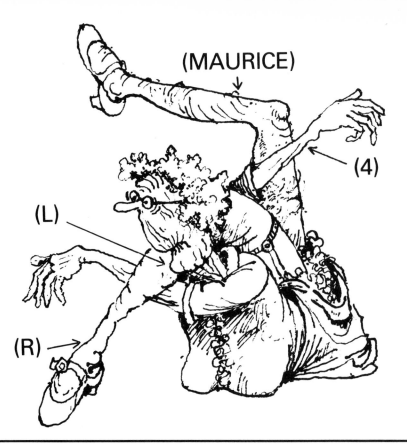

(MAURICE)

(4)

(L)

(R)

L

LATIN

A LANGUAGE SPOKEN BY DEAD ROMANS. DR FEGG HAS COMPILED HIS OWN GRAMMAR, WHICH, WHILST NOT EXACTLY EXHAUSTIVE COVERS MOST OF THE WORDS YOU NEED TO KNOW.

Amo — bullets, gunpowder, slingshot. Anything you can fire or throw.

Amas — a huge amount.

Amat — a small piece of carpet for wiping your feet on.

Amamus — a mother rodent (mouse).

Amatis — a small piece of carpet is . . .

Amant — incorrect for an ant.

Amabo — short for a motherly boa-constrictor.

Amabis — short for a motherly biscuit-constrictor (rare – *Ed.*)

Amabit — short for a motherly bit of tail (not quite as rare as you'd imagine – and *I* know – *Ed.*)

Amabimus — I don't know what this is – *Ed.*

Amabitis — a mother bit his . . .

Amabunt — short for a motherly Bunter.

Rego — to re-go somewhere, visit again.

Regis — as used in the phrase: "I'll *wreck his* flat if he comes near my wife again."

Regit — with reference to the git I was talking about.

Regimus — I don't know what this means – *Ed.*

Regitis — used with reference to specific individuals e.g. "Stanley Regit is a . . ."

Regunt — misprint for 'Regrunt' – to grunt again.

A LATIN POEM

A saila sed tumi vercani bæa frog?
Aet oldim via dua nu livdi nava bog.
E sed ædgita peni tu tacem aut again
Buta sæ tucis muni æurdit pulda chain.

A LULLABY
(a lullaby)

Uncle Fegg is far away
Doing things to sheep.
He'll come and do something
   to you,
If you don't GO TO SLEEP!

ANOTHER LULLABY
(a lullaby)

Hush, little baby
There's nothing to fear,
I'm just a child-slaughterer
Tanked up with beer.

I'm drugged to the eyeballs,
I get dizzy spells.
I'm dressed in pyjamas,
And my breath *really* smells.

But you're safe, little baby,
From razors and burns,
That's as long as I don't get
One of my "turns."

MAGIC

SOME OF DR. FEGG'S CONJURING TRICKS ARE BANNED IN CERTAIN COUNTRIES. ASK FOR A COMPLETE LIST FROM THE MAGIC CIRCLE OR FROM YOUR LOCAL POLICE STATION.

THE GREAT FEGGO! ABOUT TO PERFORM A TRICK.
The Golden Donkey Rooms, Macao, 1933.

MAGIC

Here are some wonderful tricks, just as performed by The Great Feggo, during his twenty-minute season at the Golden Donkey Rooms, Macāo in 1934.

THE DISAPPEARING GLASS

Find a friend. It doesn't matter whether you like him or not; in fact, the more he's a cross-eyed, snivelling little git whom you despise, the better. Put the friend in a box. Stand on the box and jump up and down, with a great roaring sound. If he tries to get out, tread on his fingers. That'll teach him. You can tell him you got the name of the trick wrong.

THE DISAPPEARING MATCHBOX

This is a clever one! Get a matchbox. Take all the matches out of it, and then smash it up. If the person who owns the matchbox objects, hit him over the head with whatever you're using to smash up the matchbox. For a spectacular *finale*, you can use the matches to set light to his desk. (You'll need a spare matchbox for this.) Clever, isn't it?

THE DISAPPEARING RABBIT

This is roughly the same as *The Disappearing Matchbox*, but make sure you're not anywhere near a member of the RSPCA. In fact, it's really best not to show this trick to *anybody*.

THE DISAPPEARING FRONT DOOR

For this trick you're going to need a bazooka, a bicycle chain, a crowbar, a mallet, and plenty of bandages. Ask a friend if you can go round to his house. When he says no, hit him over the head with the mallet, and tie him up with the rope (sorry, I forgot to mention the rope). When he finally invites you round, you can use the crowbar to open up the nearest parked car, and, using the skeleton keys (oh, yes – you'll need some of them, too – sorry), drive it round to his place. While he's phoning the police, you can use the wrench to force the lock on his front door, and then unscrew the hinges. (That's when you'll need the screwdriver. Forget the bicycle chain – sorry.) Put the door into the car, and push the lot over the nearest precipice. The bandages are in case you gash yourself on the jagged edges of the car door. Keep low for several weeks after this trick. Oh!... and don't forget to throw away the bazooka.

FLAGS OF ALL NATIONS

This isn't really a trick, but it's very useful to be able to do – especially if you've just done the last trick, for example. You need a set of flags of all nations that you can pull out of a hat on a single string. When you've bought one, you say to the policeman: "I'm going to take flags of all nations out of this hat on a single string!" (You'll also need a hat, of course.) And then you take out the flags of all nations on a single string out of the hat, shouting: "Hey! Flags of all nations!" and tie the policeman up with the string. At least this'll give you time to get away.

SAWING THE LADY IN HALF

I wouldn't recommend doing this trick near any populated areas. In fact, it should only be performed in total seclusion, and the more remote and inaccessible the region, the better. Try the Russian Steppes or the Ulan Bator plain. Some magicians say you should use mirrors for this trick, but I've never found them the slightest bit of help. What you need is a good sawing arm and not to be too squeamish.

THE BOURNEMOUTH KILLINGS TRICK

Dr Fegg wishes to deny all knowledge of this trick. He was in far-off Hove at the time, and in any case his firearms license expired a long time ago and the knives belonged to his uncle and were nothing to do with him at all.

MEN (Female), Great, of History

QUEEN ELIZABETH I

Queen Elizabeth the first just had to burst, but she didn't know where to do it. She'd eaten six cakes, fourteen chops, and twelve hakes, twenty rabbits, and one lump of suet. The scientists all showed that she'd probably explode if she didn't start watching her diet, but she was the Queen and she loved things with cream and she simply told them to be quiet. But it happened at last, with a voluble blast, that was heard from Devizes to Bude, and they found little bits of her Majesty's wits scattered all round the Realm in their food.

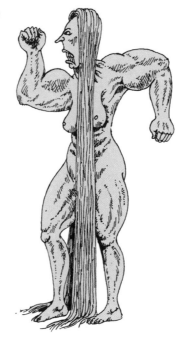

QUEEN BOADICEA

Queen Boadicea was apt to appear in a strange assortment of clothes, in things made from banana and bits of meccano and sometimes a couple of slothes. She sometimes wore mice that she filled up with rice and then hung by their tails from her waist, and each summer and fall she'd wear no clothes at all but just cover herself with meat paste. She never wore shirts or nice pleated skirts, and her subjects would often complain that a Queen should dress better than jeans and a sweater just stuffed up her nose with a crane.

LADY GODIVA

Lady Godiva would never arrive at a party or luncheon or ball; she'd never be there at a "do" with the mayor or a sale in the new Village Hall. She preferred to be home with a sizable tome called *Mechanics Made Easy for Girls*, which could teach any lass to construct or amass the machinery for conquering worlds: tanks, armoured trains, missile heads, rocket planes, and nuclear-powered spaceships as well – she was making them all so if she went to a ball, she'd be in a strong bargaining position vis-à-vis the Russians.

MEN (Male), Dr Fegg's Ten Great

There are some men who have had more than their fair share of influence over the events that shape our lives. Here is Dr Fegg's personal list of great men of our time:

1. ERNIE SWABSON

Ernie ranks high on Dr Fegg's list on account of his skill at the control and manoeuvrability of Ford Cortinas particularly on the night of March the 13th 1973.

2. "REV" WALLY SMITH

Presbyterian minister impersonator and the best look-out in the business, since "I-Spy" Cohen fell off a roof in Clapham.

3. "I-SPY" COHEN

Best look-out man in the business, till he fell off a roof in Clapham.

4. RUSS "THE GORILLA" SCREGGIT

A man with an instinctive grasp of anything he puts his hands on. Born a bricklayer, Russ worked his way up to become another bricklayer ten yards down the road. Since working for Dr Fegg, Russ has started to read books – not the right way up yet, but this will come with practice.

5. "DR" VINCE EKBERG

Demolition expert turned plastic surgeon, now a millionaire, he will always be known as the man who made the face for Dennis Healey.

6. RICKY "BAT-FACE" MOLLOY

Ricky, 37, is almost completely impervious to pain. Once, for a bet, he allowed a fully-laden 28-ton truck to be driven straight at his face. The lorry's radiator grill was buckled to a depth of 3½ feet, whilst Ricky was still able to see out of one eye.

7. PISSO, THE ALCOHOLIC DOG

A tried and trusted friend to Dr Fegg and lampposts everywhere.

MENSWEAR

How to make a Dr Fegg Casual Jacket

(i) Select four three-and-a-half-yard widths of woollen worsted.

(ii) Cut and trim the cloth to required specifications, allowing four-inch overlap at borders and seams.

(iii) Cut lapels as per pattern with two-inch border band. Pockets likewise.

(iv) Stitch in lining with double cross-stitch at seams.

(v) Assemble sleeves and jacket body with hemstitching at shoulders and match up cross-stitching at rear.

(vi) Fix buttons to cuffs and front (use matching thread).

(vii) Rip off buttons.

(viii) Pour cold tea down front and left sleeve of jacket.

(ix) Smear cooking fat (Cookeen No. 5, if possible) down lapels.

(x) Tear right hand pocket half off and insert dead mouse and/or partially set rice pudding.

(xi) Screw up jacket into as tight a ball as possible, insert in bag with three lbs. of old fish, pour in custard, tie up bag, and leave for seventeen days in dustbin.

(xii) Upwrap bag, sprinkle jacket with cigarette ash, jump up and down on it for four hours with soft-boiled eggs (three minutes) attached to soles of feet. Drop in toilet and flush it.

Your Dr Fegg casual jacket is now ready to wear.

N.B.: If you are disappointed with the results, remember that all clothes look a little new to start with, but it'll soon wear in.

To make a Dr Fegg Dinner Jacket for more formal occasions: Follow directions, as above, but use crushed otter's entrails instead of custard.

MUSICAL INSTRUMENTS (History of)

PREHISTORIC TIMES

The first musical instrument was a bit of wood with a nail in it. The soloist used this to hit the nearest passer-by, thus producing a note of a certain pitch. Experiments were made by hitting passers-by with different sized bits of wood, but the pitch of the note was always unpredictable. However they did eventually develop a variable pitch instrument in which the player lined up his whole family and hit them one by one. Each member of the family would produce a different note. Unfortunately this instrument was eventually outlawed owing to the interfering wets at the Humane Music Appreciation Society, who wouldn't recognise a good idea if it hit them on the head. I know 'cause I've tried.

ANCIENT EGYPT

The Egyptians' favourite musical instrument was the Liar. It consisted of a hard-boiled egg, some old underwear and a packet of Benson & Hedges. You squashed the hard-boiled egg up with the fag-ends and placed them in the underpants. Then you showed them to a concert-goer, who would produce an interesting sliding scale of notes on the theme of "Urrgh."

ROMAN TIMES

This was the heyday of musical appre-ciation. Roman music was particularly violent. Recently archeological discoveries have revealed musical instruments of fiendish ingenuity.

The Lip Pipe. This instrument was inserted into the mouth and blown in the manner of a shawm (see below). Once placed in the mouth, however, it was impossible to remove, and those who took up the lip pipe never played anything else (or ate or drank again).

The Paino. The soloist is entirely encased in a globe of spikes which revolves as he plays, causing extreme anguish and horror. Solos were kept short but frequent. On festival days bets would be taken on which painoplayer would last out an entire performance.

The Roman Bagpipe. The instrumen-talist was forced into the bag and then stuffed into a narrow pipe which was, in turn, placed over a fire. The low moaning tone of this instrument was said to have made it a favourite of Agrippa (Marcus Vipsanius 63–12 B.C.).

The Fiddle. The Roman Fiddle was basically the same as the modern violin, except for the spike. *

The Flute. This was *not* very popular with the Romans as it did not injure the player at all and produced rather pleasant sounds.

* This was driven into the chin to keep the instrument in place.

THE MIDDLE AGES

In the Middle Ages music went into a decline. Hardly anyone died from music, and even maiming and stunning played a less and less important role in musical technique. The only exceptions were:

The Shawm. Basically a forerunner of the oboe, it could be bent round the soloist's neck in the normal way.

The Crumhorn. Caught in the player's nostril, and jerked upwards sharply, this could be a useful instrument in its way. But its popularity has been overtaken completely by the Vibraphone (*see* below).

THE MODERN DAY

The Vibraphone. This is the only modern instrument worth talking about. Even drumsticks are padded nowadays, but with the Vibraphone you still get hammers that can inflict a certain amount of personal injury, although even this is pretty minimal. Hence the development, by the pioneering Dr Fegg, of . . .

The Feggophone. A short, fat blunt instrument delivering a kick like a horse. The instrument is held, lightly but firmly, by three men in helmets. The Feggophonist should then lay his right-hand forefinger lightly on the 'A' key (or "trigger") and blow into the mouthpiece ("detonator"). Within seconds a hail of untreated sewage will cover any audience within a range of 300 yards (which means you can play the largest halls).

The Pentagon already have six on order, and a Kosher version is being developed for the Middle East.

Concert

The Nasty Symphony/Fegg
Festival Hall

Dr Fegg's Nasty Symphony in J-flat received its first performance behind London's Festival Hall last night. It was an extraordinary occasion. Dr Fegg, the composer, claims to have had no formal musical training, and there were few there last night who would dispute this, as he put the cello to his lips for the so-called first movement. The sharp sound of splintering wood against teeth, as Dr Fegg took his first bite of the beautiful 200-year-old instrument, counterpointed with the low groans of the 200-year-old cellist from the Royal Philharmonic, lying bound and gagged behind the dustbins, and now coming round for the first time. The *adagio molto sostenuto* passage came to a sharp climax with the sound of a single horn, as Dr Fegg brought it down on the head of the elderly cellist, now rising unsteadily to his feet. A cry, *f. fortissimo*, and the first movement was at an end.

The second movement (*molto presto*) commenced with all the bustle and excitement of a *Scherzo*, as the onlookers surged forward to restrain Dr Fegg, who was, by now, making full use of the timpani to beat up yet another partially concussed member of the Royal Philharmonic. Fegg turned, and the faintly musical crunch of harp on bone as he hurled an elegant Louis XV lyre at his first assailant served as an effective introduction to the strings, with which he was soon lashing out wildly in all directions, stunning and maiming men and women on both sides as they tried to get at him.

The third and final movement of the Nasty Symphony was a triumph. It began softly with the distant wail of the siren and, as Dr Fegg, *con fuoco*, threw xylophone after xylophone through the windows of the nearby Festival Hall, the siren grew closer and suddenly we were back in the main *allegro* ... but *risoluto* this time. The marvellous entry of the police counterpointed subtly by the whining D-minor protestations of Dr Fegg himself, followed by the delightful opening of the doors of the van in squeaky counterpoint and then the majestic climax – the final repetition of Dr Fegg's earlier theme of violent personal abuse, coupled with the surge of power from the van's engine and the final echoing cry of the police siren itself. For those of us who were privileged to watch the Nasty Symphony, a night in the cells was a small price to pay.

Bernard Feggin

DEATHS BY MUSIC

Comparative Chart of Musical Deaths through the Ages.

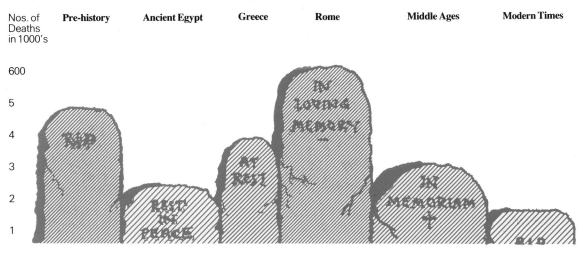

Nos. of Deaths in 1000's	Pre-history	Ancient Egypt	Greece	Rome	Middle Ages	Modern Times
600						
5						
4						
3						
2						
1						

NEWSPAPERS

Useful for wrapping up fish and concealing things from the Japanese. Here is a bit found in Dr Fegg's shoe whilst searching for rats (see **Pantomime**).

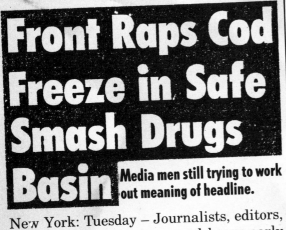

Front Raps Cod Freeze in Safe Smash Drugs Basin

Media men still trying to work out meaning of headline.

New York: Tuesday – Journalists, editors, and sub-editors spent several hours early today in a futile attempt to resolve the meaning of one of their headlines. But despite all efforts, it remains a meaningless jumble (continued on p.32).

TODAY'S WEATHER

Sunny spells.

Warm and generally pleasant; but light rain spreading from the east later in the day, followed by enormous dark clouds, terrifically noisy thunder, great big ear-shattering frighteningly huge bright red flashes of lightning, hailstones the size of pastrami sandwiches, followed by glaciers, volcanoes, enormous upheavals of the earth's crust, huge gaps a mile wide, strange creatures with eighteen eyes in each leg and the power of nine million bulldozers, followed in late evening by world domination for Fegg! *Tomorrow: Showers and sunny periods.*

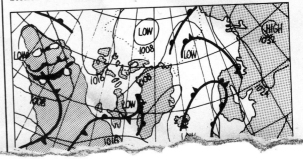

What to do in the event of Nuclear War

Write or call FEGG ENTERPRISES for the one *sure* way to avoid immolation and certain death – a **GENUINE** invitation to join a nuclear shelter club . . .

I hereby apply to join my nearest

NUCLEAR SHELTER CLUB

I understand that if Nuclear War breaks out I shall be amongst the Few Who Are Saved.

NAME & ADDRESS ....
....
....

NAME & ADDRESS OF BANK
....
....

CREDIT CARDS: (If 'Gold' Card Owner, please state) ....

NAME & ADDRESS OF CLUB ......
....
....

NAME & ADDRESS OF SCHOOL
....

TYPE OF ACCENT (e.g. Harrovian, Sandhurst, Slightly Cockney [cf. Michael Caine] Unbearably Cockney [Taxi-Drivers])

HAVE YOU AT ANY TIME IN YOUR LIFE BEEN TO BED WITH DR KISSINGER? ....

IF A NUCLEAR WAR BREAKS OUT WHOSE FAULT WILL IT BE? *(Please cross out where non-applicable)*
(a) The Free World's
(b) Entirely the Russians'

£99.95

COMPLETE WITH GLASS

I understand that if I am selected to join the NUCLEAR SHELTER CLUB I will not smoke cheap cigarettes, bring any books by E. P. Thompson, be rude about Trust House Forte's in-shelter catering or whistle Joni Mitchell songs. I also undertake to always abide by the solemn oath of the Nuclear Shelter Club.

THE OATH OF THE NUCLEAR SHELTER CLUB:
I solemnly undertake that I, as a member of the NUCLEAR SHELTER CLUB, will never at any time state, write or by another means employ the phrase "I told you so".

Tear off and send *(as fast as you can)* to:-

NUCLEAR SHELTER CLUB LTD., c/o AIMS OF INDUSTRY
The Bed Department, Harrods.

Tea with Uncle Fegg

Uncle Fegg, oh, Uncle Fegg,
What are you doing there?
A chicken in your trousers
And porridge in your hair?

Why are you throwing rats at me?
And kicking that poor goat?
Why have you leapt upon me thus
And gripped me by the throat?

Why do you bang my head so much
Upon the bathroom floor?
Why have you got the carving knife?
And what's that bucket for?

Oh! Uncle Fegg! Oh! Uncle Fegg!
It really seems to me,
That it was all a BIG MISTAKE
To ask you round for tea. . . .

Simple Simon

Simple Simon
Met a Pieman
Selling poisoned pies.
Said the pieman
"Why not try one?"
As he brushed off the flies.
Said Simple Simon
"Thank you, pieman,"
And died, to his surprise.

Jack and Jill

Jack and Jill went up the hill
To fetch a pail of water.
Jack fell down
And grabbed Jill as he fell,
Jack was all right,
But they found Jill at the bottom
    of the quarry three days later.

Daffodils and Flowers
by Laurence the Poet

Daffodils go ping! and oink!
They really are alarming!
I'm scared of big geraniums
And I'm sure that lilac's harming!

I don't feel safe with primroses
And pansies make me jump!
A rhododendron bush makes me go
    all wobbly.
And I'm terrified that hyacinths
    might whop me when I'm not looking!
Oh dear, just talking about it
makes me want to go and sit down.

OBSERVATION

Test your powers of observation by looking at these two pictures. If you can see them that's a start. Now look more carefully.

Somewhere in these two pictures there are certain differences. If you look hard, you *may* spot them. Write them down and time yourself. **Less than three minutes:** very bright indeed. **Less than ten minutes:** jolly clever. **Less than an hour:** still jolly clever, though perhaps not quite up to scholarship standard, (but who cares about silly old scholarships, anyway!) **Over four hours:** well done! Even *quite good* atom scientists were slow starters. **Ten to twelve days:** a very good try indeed! **Over four months:** keep at it! **Four months to one year:** you're doing well!

WHICH PICTURE GOES WITH WHICH?

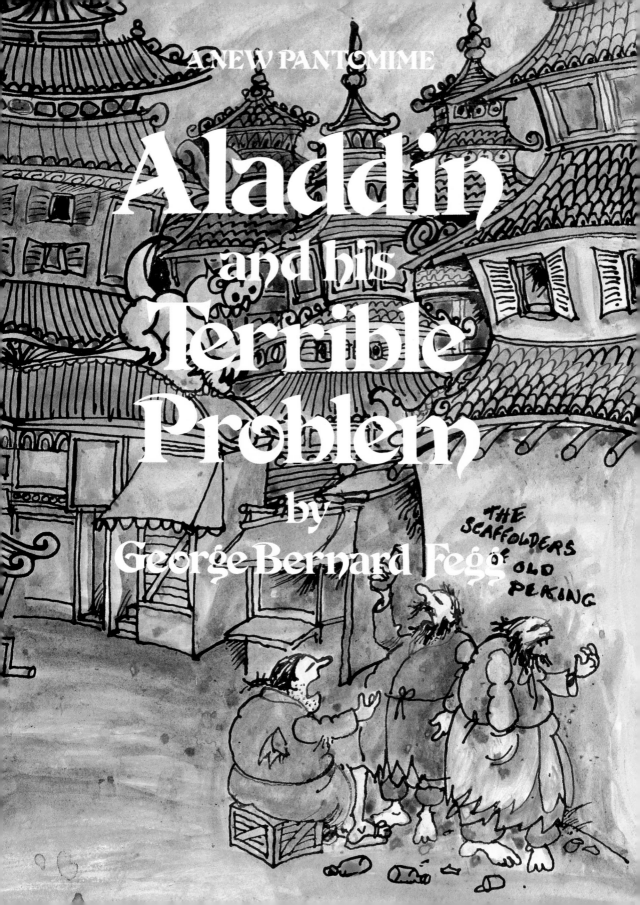

A NEW PANTOMIME

Aladdin
and his
Terrible
Problem

by

George Bernard Fegg

THE SCAFFOLDERS OF OLD PEKING

Characters in Order of Appearance

Aladdin
A young Chinese boy/girl

Widow Twankey
A Chinese washerwoman

The Rev. Wishee Washee
An English clergyman

Pisso
An alcoholic dog

Vic Danzigger *A man pledged
to the destruction of Depravo*

The Emperor of China
An emperor of China

Ming and Mong *Policemen*

Rutherford and Morgan
Wishee Washee's solicitors

Depravo the Rat
A friend of Pisso's

Princess Lucky *The Emperor's daughter*

Puss *Princess Lucky's constant companion*

Simon the Vet *The man who neutered Puss*

Abanazar *A magician*

**Filthy Philip,
the Unhygenic Hedgehog** *A friend of Pisso's*

John Cole *A political correspondent and friend of Pisso's*

Violet Kaunda *A Zambian President's cousin*

Scaffolders of Old Peking

The National Health Choir

AND INTRODUCING
The Amazing Bert Fegg ⨯ 2 *Death-Defying High-Wire Act*

Act One

SCENE ONE

The Barclaycard Centre, Northampton.
Enter ALADDIN. *He looks very unhappy.*

ALADDIN. Oh I'm so unhappy! Today I saw. . . .

A BARCLAYCARD REPRESENTATIVE. I'm sorry. Have you. . . .

ALADDIN. Today I saw the Princess in her room in the castle, and I wanted to. . . .

A BARCLAYCARD REPRESENTATIVE. If you have an enquiry, will you please ask at the desk.

      ORCHESTRA *begins.*

A BARCLAYCARD REPRESENTATIVE. *Please!* This is our central accounting department. No unauthorized personnel. . . .

ALADDIN [*sings*].   Princess I love you
                        Oh yes I do!
                        Princess I do love
                        You.

    Enter CHORUS *of* CHINESE BOYS *and* GIRLS, SCAFFOLDERS, *and* WAITERS *(the back row of whom could be Italian).*

A BARCLAYCARD REPRESENTATIVE. *Please!*

ALADDIN *and* CHORUS [*singing*]. All day long I think of you
                                  Princess, you're the one!

    ALADDIN *jumps onto an F 278B computer.*

    The BOYS, GIRLS, SCAFFOLDERS, *and* WAITERS *stand on expensive adding equipment and gaze at* ALADDIN *in sympathy.*

ALADDIN [*singing*].   You're my extra special love
                        My only one.

    Enter MR ATKINS *and* MR TALBOT, *security men, together with* MEMBERS OF THE NORTHAMPTONSHIRE CONSTABULARY, *led by* A BARCLAYCARD REPRESENTATIVE.

ALADDIN [*still singing*].   Tho' you'll never know my name –

A BARCLAYCARD REPRESENTATIVE [*pointing at* ALADDIN]. That's him!

ALADDIN [*still singing*].   I love you all the same.

A NORTHAMPTONSHIRE POLICEMAN. Come along, sir.

ALADDIN [*jumping onto a sensitive data storage processor and still singing*]. For your heart I'll always aim.

A NORTHAMPTONSHIRE POLICEMAN. This is private property.

ALADDIN [*sings*].   My. . . .Princess!

    ORCHESTRA *goes on playing the refrain.*

A fight has broken out between SECURITY MEN *and* SCAFFOLDERS OF OLD PEKING.
MR ATKINS' *nose is broken.*

CHORUS [*singing*]. Tho' you'll never know my name –

MR ATKINS. You swivel-eyed git!

He punches one of the SCAFFOLDERS. *He ducks.* MR ATKINS *hits one of* ALADDIN'S
YOUNG FRIENDS.

CHORUS [*singing*]. I love you all the same.

INSPECTOR BARRET *of the Northampton C.I.D. intervenes to stop* MR ATKINS
assaulting another CHINESE GIRL.

CHORUS [*singing*]. For your heart I'll always aim.

CHORUS *are led away by the* POLICE. *One of the* WAITERS *has been partially scalped.*

CHORUS [*singing as best they can*]. My. . .Princess!

SCENE TWO

Back in Old Peking.

The SCAFFOLDERS *and* YOUNG CHINESE GIRLS *are playing around a well in the
marketplace. One of the* SCAFFOLDERS *has a plaster over his lower lip. Enter*
ALADDIN *and* PISSO. ALADDIN *still looks very sad.* PISSO *is staggering slightly.*

ALADDIN. Oh, Pisso! What am I to do? Everyone's so happy except me.

PISSO *falls against the side of the well.*

ALADDIN. Pisso, my good old friend. Tell me what I can do to make the Princess love
me.

PISSO *tries to get up, but his front legs give way and he slumps down again beside the
well.*

ALADDIN. Oh, Pisso! Have you been at it again?

SONG: *"Pisso's Been at It Again"*

ALADDIN [*sings*].   Well, most dogs like a nice big bone
                                     Its jelly makes them frisky.
                                     But Pisso likes a glass of beer
                                     Four brandies and a whiskey.

CHORUS [*singing*].   Oh, Pisso's been at it again.
                                     If he's had one he's had ten!
                                     For breakfast he has lager beer,
                                     For lunch it's gin and wine.
                                     And we always know where Pisso is
                                     When it comes to opening time.
                                     Oh, Pisso's been at it again.
                                     He's worse than a duck or a hen!

When he comes in late at night
And starts talking to the light
We all know. . . .
Pisso's been at it again!

Trumpets sound off. Enter THE EMPEROR OF CHINA, PRINCESS LUCKY, *and* ATTENDANT CHIROPODISTS.

ALADDIN The Princess! Oh, Pisso, quick!

ALADDIN *rushes to the side of the stage and hides.* PISSO *is left in the market square. He tries to get up but his paws crumple beneath him and he falls over onto his side.*

ALADDIN [*urgently*]. Pisso!

PISSO *pulls himself up on his front two legs. His eyes go misty and he is sick behind the well.*

ALADDIN, THE SCAFFOLDERS, *and the* YOUNG CHINESE GIRLS *look on in horror.*

EMPEROR. What is this? What creature dares to soil the marketplace of Old Peking?

PISSO *belches and brings up his dinner.*

EMPEROR. Chiropodists! Seize him!

The CHIROPODISTS *rush forwards and try to seize* PISSO *without getting too dirty.* PISSO *tries to make a break for it, but he falls and rolls over into the gutter.*

EMPEROR. Chiropodists! Execute him forthwith! [*To* PISSO] Have you a solicitor?

PISSO *groans.*

EMPEROR. Good! We won't have to go through all that trial business. Off with his. . . .

ALADDIN *rushes out and prostrates himself in front of the* EMPEROR.

ALADDIN. Please! Save Pisso! Kill me instead!

One of the CHIROPODISTS *steps forward and kills* ALADDIN.

EMPEROR [*to* CHIROPODIST]. You fool!

CURTAIN

END OF ACT ONE

Act Two

SCENE ONE

A dungeon in the Palace, ALADDIN'S STAND-IN *is gazing mournfully out of the window. He looks very unhappy.* PISSO *is slumped in the corner.*

ALADDIN'S STAND-IN [*rubbing his neck ruefully*]. Oh, Pisso, my head doesn't half hurt where I had it chopped off.

PISSO *groans and starts to cough.*

ALADDIN'S STAND-IN. Oh, Pisso! What *are* we going to do? Here we are in prison, the Princess thinks I am a common criminal. I may never see her again. Oh! If *only* I had a solicitor. . . .

      PISSO *is racked by a severe cough.*

ALADDIN'S STAND-IN. Have *you* got a solicitor, Pisso?

      PISSO *reaches inside his anti-eczema collar and produces a crumpled visiting-card.*
      He pushes it towards ALADDIN'S STAND-IN. ALADDIN'S STAND-IN *reads it.*

ALADDIN'S STAND-IN. Oh no! Not him! Not *him*, Pisso!

      PISSO *whines wretchedly.*

ALADDIN'S STAND-IN. I am *not* employing Depravo the Rat.

SCENE TWO

    Inside DEPRAVO'S *lair. It is full of half-eaten food, and flies buzz around it.*
    DEPRAVO *is rubbing a bare patch on his skin up against a brick wall, and singing the while.*
    SONG: *"I'm Depravo, Depravo the Rat"*

DEPRAVO [*sings*].   I'm Depravo, Depravo the Rat,
                  As filthy a creature as can be.
                  I'm vicious and ill-tempered,
                  I make everybody jump,
                  I cheat and lie and swindle,
                  And smell like a rubbish dump.
                  I haven't got a heart of gold,
                  I've no redeeming feature,
                  I'm Depravo the Rat,
                  A truly filthy creature.

    BITS OF UNEATEN FOOD, COCKROACHES, *and* SCAFFOLDERS *sing.*

CHORUS.   He's Depravo. . . .Depravo the Rat
                  The biggest health hazard in Peking.

DEPRAVO.   I like being very rude,
                  Eating half-digested food
                  And seeing ladies in the nude.

ALL.   He's Depravo, Depravo the Rat
                  As filthy a creature as could be.
                  He hasn't got a heart of gold,
                  He's no redeeming feature,
                  He's Depravo the Rat,
                  A truly filthy creature.

CHORUS.	Even slimy little toads
	When girls look in their minces
	Tend to go all soppy
	And turn into handsome Princes.
DEPRAVO.	But there's no chance of that
	With Depravo the Rat.
	I'm a loose-living, dirty little scab.
	So keep away, do-gooders,
	Don't come being nice to me,
	Or I'll make your life real hell.
	I'll slit your face
	And wet your bed,
	I'll wrap your nostrils round your head.
ALL.	He's Depravo, Depravo the Rat,
	As filthy a creature as could be,
	He hasn't changed his underpants since 1923.
	He's Depravo the Rat.
DEPRAVO.	The filthiest creature. . . .
CHORUS.	The filthiest creature. . . .
ALL.	The filthiest creature there could be!

CURTAIN

END OF ACT TWO

Theatre goes out of business

Other works for the theatre by G. B. Fegg

It Didn't Happen in Bournemouth   Staying Away From The South Coast
No Footprints in June   Look Back in Panic

Classical Works Starring Depravo the Rat

King Lear

PARLOUR GAMES

PASS THE BENGAL TIGER

Requirements:

Seven boys, seven girls, fourteen chairs, piano, wrapping paper, one Bengal tiger.

Object of the Game:

To avoid being left holding the Bengal tiger (for obvious reasons).

How to Play:

Ask your mother or an Auntie (whoever you will miss least) to wrap up a Bengal tiger in brown paper. Then sit around on the fourteen chairs – boys and girls alternately. When the music starts, pass the Bengal tiger around (if you can!). Whoever is left holding the Bengal tiger when the music stops (Good luck to you!) must unwrap one of the pieces of paper around the legendary, vicious brute. When the music starts, you must immediately pass the Bengal tiger on (not that you'll need much persuading!) to the person next to you. The person who takes the last piece of paper off the Bengal tiger is deemed to be the loser, and is bitten to death by the now-enraged mammal. The winners all get sweeties and a quiet lie down.

HOW TO THROW SHADOWS ON THE WALL

SPOONS

Requirements:

Seven boys, seven girls, fourteen chairs, piano, a dozen spoons, one Bengal tiger.

Object of the Game:

To collect as many spoons as possible before being killed.

How to Play:

The spoons are laid out in various parts of the room by your mother or an Auntie (whoever's left). On the command, "Go!" the boys and girls must try and pick up as many spoons as possible whilst the Bengal tiger runs amok.

WARNING: Do NOT play this game if you have any valuable furniture or precious ornaments in the room.

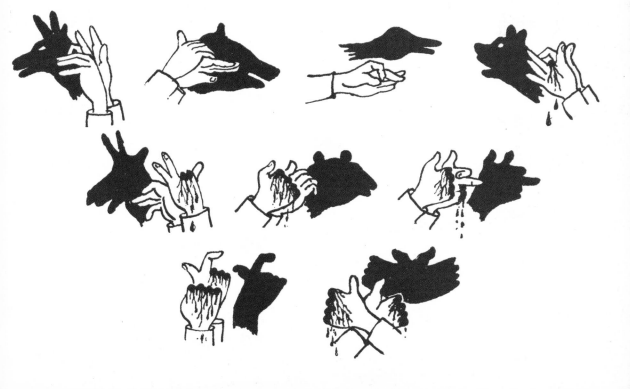

PSYCHIATRY, a doctor inquires

HOW MAD AM I?

1. When you wake up in the morning, do you?
A. Feel relaxed, comfortable and happy?
B. Feel tense, anxious, depressed?
C. Recite the Beveridge Report in a high-pitched whine changing the word "and" to "swollen" every time it occurs?

2. Do you look forward to your work?
A. Yes, very much.
B. Not particularly.
C. Loopy-oo-do-dum diddle I day-o!

3. Personal Relationships – Would you say that you have
A. A friend to whom you can tell everything?
B. No friend to whom you can tell everything?
C. A section of the Thames Barrage to whom you can tell everything?

4. When someone sneezes would you advise them to
A. Apologise?
B. Sneeze again, only more loudly?
C. Seek psychiatric help?

5. If someone, who has a phobia about Fried Chicken, came to see you – would you
A. Laugh?
B. Find out about their childhood?
C. Charge them £300?

SCORE

1. A – 10   B – 5   C – 0
2. A – 10   B – 5   C – 0
3. A – 10   B – 5   C – 0
4. A – 10   B – 5   C – 0
5. A – 10   B – 5   C – 0

HOW DID YOU SCORE?
50 – You are sick and need immediate help.
25 – You are perfectly normal, apart from the herpes.
0 – Congratulations! You are a fully qualified psychiatrist. Please ring and collect badge and free bucket!

QUESTIONS

Questions are those things you usually try to avoid answering, especially if they are being put to you by people in helmets, and are prefaced by the words 'Hey! You!'. Here are some of the few questions with which Dr Fegg is familiar, which do not mention Bournemouth or the whereabouts of the blunt instrument.

1. What's finger-lickin' unpleasant?
Answer: Kentucky-Fried Fegg.

2. What plays Mozart at the same time it hacks your legs off?
Answer: The Royal Philharmonic Fegg.

DR FEGG'S EASY ANAGRAMS

1. A
2. LBOOD
3. BLODO
4. EMOR BLODO
5. BUKCETS OF BLODO
6. BLODO NRUNING DWON ETH SEDIS OF ETH BUKCETS
7. BLODO ALL OVRE ETH CAPRET
8. DAETH PENALTY

Answers to the Easy Anagrams

1. A
2. BLODO
3. B DOOR MOLE
4. BLEST DUCK OF OBO
5. NO DOG IS LIKE OUR BEN BUT WHO NEEDS THFDNS
6. ALL THAT BOLD CREEPER OOV
7. THE ANT PLAYED

QUIZZES

An entertainment in which the general or specific knowledge of the players is tested by a series of questions.

Here is a selection specially devised by Dr Fegg to while away those endless months of waiting (totally unjustifiably).

Dr Fegg's Quiz

1. Which American President was called McKinley?
2. Which world leader
3. Complete question 2 and answer it as best you can.
4. Doctor Fegg has a hamster. Is it:
(a) alive?
(b) dead?
5. Doctor Fegg likes his bath:
(a) very hot.
(b) quite hot.
(c) once every 3 years.
6. Would you describe Dr Fegg's Quiz of All World Knowledge as:
(a) a waste of time?
(b) a good idea badly presented?
(c) excellent and informative?
7. Can Emus answer the phone?
Yes / No / Not sure / Well. . . / I don't *think* so / Perhaps / *Emus?*
8. A *monsoon* is:
(a) an anagram.
(b) a terribly twee little plaster ornament with a picture of Dwight Eisenhower on one side and a photo of a half-open fir cone on the other.
(c) the answer to question 7.
9. The Taj Mahal is:
(a) a very hot curry based on onions and coriander.
(b) a club in Wigan.
(c) an enormous hairbrush with a white dome and patterned marble walls inlaid with precious jewels, in a graceful fusion of Islamic and Indian styles.
10. Which famous world statesmen are lit up at night, and where?
(a) Henry Kissinger (who is also a doctor).
(b) Rod Stewart.
(c) Dr David Owen (who is also a politician).
11. Dr Fegg wrote which of the following great novels:
(a) *War and Peace*
(b) *The Tale of Two Cities*
(c) *The Nasty Babysitter*

Answers on page 79 of 'Fisherman's Weekly' (August, 1961)

HISTORY AND POLITICS QUIZ

1. Which of the following Famous World Leaders needs money quick?

1   2   3   4

Answer: No 4 – and hurry!

2. In what year did the following take place?

Answer: Not available for security reasons

3. Are the police still looking for Dr Fegg?
Answer: If you know the answer to this question, write it IN BLOCK CAPITALS and leave in a plain envelope Behind the Hot Water Pipes In the Gentlemen's Rest Room Victoria Station (along with the money for question 1).

4. Has Interpol been brought in yet?
Answer: To be left with the answer to question 3. And don't forget the money.

5. Where would *you* go if you had to lie low for a bit, and bearing in mind that Basingstoke is only just up the road?
1. Bahamas
2. Guatemala
3. Peru
4. Basingstoke
5. Split
Answer: Leave the answer with 3 and 4. Any other suggestions welcome.

6. Have *you* ever used any of the following weapons?
Answer: If the answer is "yes," write at once to Inspector Phillips, The Vicarage, Ashton-under-Lyne, England. You will be surprised how interested he will be to hear from you.

QUIZZES (2)

A maze for people who don't like to get confused

Dr Fegg's range of fascinating sweets for kiddies...

MURDER MICE

As you go to bite their eyes, *they* bite *you!*

Self-Abuse Rock

Gob & Throat Stoppers

SMARTIES

that really *do* make you smart! *Cannot* be washed off!

CAMBODO CHEWS

Dark rich chocolate with soft centres filled with one of the world's finest defoliants

'Bust-your-Gut' NOUGAT

Completely impervious to all digestive juices. The nougat, once eaten, simply remains in the stomach for ever.

RADIOACTIVE SHERBERT

"Melts the Mouth"

HORROR BON-BONS

Impossible to remove from the hand.

HANG YOURSELF GUM

Throw-up Drops

LIQUORICE ALL-SORTS

All sorts of shapes *and* sizes and poses! For all free-thinking youngsters!

Available now - so hurry! hurry! before the police get there . . .

HOW THEY LIVED IN ROMAN TIMES

ROME (Ancient)

You are about to visit the house of one of Dr Fegg's ancestors. His name is Titus Fegg and he is a moderately well-off citizen living in Rome around the year 110 AD.

1 Shop let to cousin Typhus Fegg, where he sells soft drinks and ice-creams, "herbal remedies" under the motto "Unum probate nullam ultram necessitatum habete" (once you've tried one you'll never need another).

2 ATRIUM where visitors are frisked, relieved of uncomfortable objects such as wallets, bags of gold and

Imagine you have been transported back 2000 years

so on, before being invited to "get lost" or being thrown into the IMPLUVIUM.

3 IMPLUVIUM or rubbish dump. A useful place to store old bones and general refuse.

4 VOMITORIUM. The biggest room in the house. It is here that Titus Fegg and his friends relax after a hard day's eating and drinking.

5 CONDUIT into main "sewer" or "thoroughfare". Note the passers-by checking the time of day by the contents of the sewer.

6 TABLINUM. Here Titus Fegg greets visitors and harangues them for many hours about his belief in capital punishment for children and the need to put more rats in school meals. From here the visitor may hurry on into the PERISTYLE.

7 PERISTYLE. In this shaded cloister surrounding the DILAPIDARIUM, (reserve rubbish tip), the visitor, followed by his host, will learn of Titus's desire to provide free axes for psychopaths, his scheme to import rabid dogs, his dream of giving all orphans six hours to leave the country, and of allowing all slaves no matter how menial to be able to work through the night.

8 SERVANTS' QUARTERS. From here, the visitor will be prevented from examining the servants' quarters, where a slave is being punished for being fair-haired.

9 BEDROOMS. The visitor will also be invited not to go up to the sleeping quarters, where Titus' young nephew and his one-legged tutor are learning their latest lesson.

10 SOLARIUM. If the visitor is an old friend or an important official or if he simply gives his host the rest of the money that he'd hidden under his toga, he may be shown the solarium, where Titus keeps his best garbage. Some he has kept since childhood, and to stroll round this special room is to be taken on a trip back through Titus' life: from the complete collection of his early nappies right through to the remains of last night's supper, and what the dog did on one of the cushions.

11 TRICLINIUM. Finally the honoured guest may be ushered into the Triclinium. Stepping over the dead body of a servant who though apparently dark-haired turned out to have a fairish patch on his chest when examined during supper, he will find himself in a room of surprising luxury. The walls are decorated with eight-legged chairs made entirely of caviar, on the floor there is a carpet woven by specially trained goldfish from the chest-hair of Egyptian ambassadors, and early theodolites crackle merrily on the fire. The ceiling is covered in representations of the passing seasons carved from the nasal bridges of female tapirs.

The dinner party reclines under the comfortable couches, while Titus flings rare and exotic food at them, and servants pour wine from stone jars onto their heads.

The end of the evening is usually signalled by Titus, himself, falling in a stupor over the body of the last servant who, though dark-haired, happened to let slip that he had an uncle in Ostva who couldn't really see anything wrong with fair hair. The guests tiptoe out, paying over their last few gold coins to the door-keeper, before running home and bolting the door.

RUNNING

Running is good for your health. Try running a couple of miles before breakfast. Everyone else will be in the exercise yard, so you should get at least a three-minute start. Dr Fegg, with his long interest in all aspects of physical well-being, has designed the following accessories which you may find useful.

The 'Terriermatic' False Dog

An almost lifelike automatic dog. Though its outward appearance is being constantly modified and improved the sight of this 17-foot long, stainless-steel poodle fouling the pavement can give you vital seconds of surprise.

'Meat-O-Squirt'

Invaluable for the really desperate runner, Essence of Mutton in a tastefully packaged aerosol spray, which can be instantly applied to walls, chimneys and fences guaranteed to delay all dogs for a minimum of forty seconds – and really stupid ones for up to five days.

The 'Spring-U-Quik' telescopic ladder

For the man who finds starting the hardest bit. Extends from an uncannily lifelike 9 × 8 cm Kupcake into a 40-foot aluminium ladder. Sir Robert Mark says 'At last a positive contribution to the problem of overcrowded prisons.'

The 'Runner's Friend'

A heavy-duty industrial grease which, if liberally applied over your 'running' uniform, should help put off the runners behind you from catching up and trying to persuade you to get into their van.

SATELLITES

With the exciting developments in New Technology, more and more satellites are being sent into orbit which can bring interstellar research into your own home. These are some of the exciting possibilities.

1. The 'Watch-A-Pal' Personal Surveillance Satellite

Now! Thanks to the miracle of sophisticated, ultra high-frequency beam response you can hear what people say about you after you've left the room! How much should those strawberries have really cost? Does your breath smell? Are your views on education as dull as they sound? Find out if people really like you – by satellite.

2. The 'Hygena' Maxi Clens Personal Satellite

Developed by international dry-cleaners from the infra-red capabilities of the ORBITER weather satellites, the Hygena Maxi Clens will give you a hygiene print-out of your body *before* you leave for the office: heavy perspiration areas in blue, unwashed dirt in red, pimple risk areas in yellow. *Also* useful on your clothes. Infra-red camera will photograph, and instantly process your appearance – right through to your knickers, revealing stains, creases, and potential holes. Also built in micro-alarm which sounds if clothes have been worn for more than five days (inner garments) or three weeks (outer garments).

3. The Masters and Johnson 'Sex' Satellite

Guaranteed to change your whole attitude to small mammals. If you've a sex problem, simply pick up your telephone when the satellite is in your area and breathe heavily. Either Dr Masters or Dr Johnson will immediately materialise and tell you what you're doing wrong and how cross God would be if he knew and how to get your leg down *off* it. They will then offer you personal advice and leave discreetly by the back door. On no account should you follow procedures for Satellite 3 and go outside and lie down with your mouth open.

*The long-awaited launch of FEGG 8, the so-called 'nasty' satellite, has been postponed once again due to lack of a suitable milk bottle. When FEGG 8 is fully operational it will broadcast video-nasties 24 hours a day from a height of 12 feet – so watch out!

4. THE DENT-U-STICK SATELLITE

Picks your teeth spotlessly clean with a powerful laser beam. Guaranteed to get out even the most difficult bits of bacon, old pieces of masonry – anything lodged between either incisors or molars is instantly vaporised, leaving the mouth *refreshed* and only slightly charred. Simply dial the number, go outside onto flat, open ground and lie down with your mouth open.

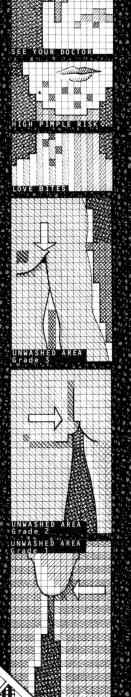

SEE YOUR DOCTOR

HIGH PIMPLE RISK

LOVE BITES

UNWASHED AREA
Grade 3

UNWASHED AREA
Grade 2

UNWASHED AREA
Grade 1

ATHLETES FOOT

SCOUTING

Dr Fegg has long been interested in boys in shorts. He has now compiled the first all-new scouting manual since Frank Sinatra* founded the movement. *Fegg's Scouting Manual* teaches you:

FRANK SINATRA*

*Sorry. This should read Frank Sinatra, later Lord Baden-Powell.

How to help old ladies halfway across the road.

How to put up a tent.

How to put up a cheap but functional apartment block.

How to put up a Holiday Inn.

How to start a fire using only kerosene.

How to get odd looks by rubbing two sticks together.

How to follow a trail.

How to make an arrest.

How to be a witness.

How to be a member of a jury.

How to get a quick verdict.

How to join a Citizens' Action Group.

How to have a gun always ready

How to run for Parliament on a law and order ticket.

How to give an acceptance address to 10,000 people.

How to become interested in firm government.

How to become interested in torchlight processions,

How to invade Belgium.

Fegg's Scouting Manual also includes his new Boy Scout motto

(To be repeated every six minutes, with two fingers on a badger.)

I admire Dr Fegg and all he stands for. If he is ever in trouble, I will be by his side, or failing that, get my parents to send him money.**

DR FEGG'S GUIDE TO CAMPING

1. Camping is a wet, uncomfortable, and miserable way to die, but, if you can't avoid it, you can at least make it comfortable.

2. Select your camping spot carefully. Very often, you will find people in tents and caravans blocking your view and generally getting in the way. These can usually be dispersed by naming your dog *Cholera* and calling him in loudly last thing at night.

3. Once you have found a nice spot, get out the flame-thrower and clear the area around you.

4. What you will need for a Camping Trip:

4,286 9" by 3" bricks	*Window frames*
12 sacks Easy-Drying Ready-Mixed Cement	*Plate glass*
	Stereo equipment
Front door	*Carpets, various*
Back door	*Slates*
Porch	*Roofing timbers*
Piano	*Second piano*
Chairs	*(if room)*

5. Pack these carefully – with the plate glass *at the top.*

6. Get someone else to carry the pack.

7. Camp.

ALTERNATIVES TO CAMPING

1. Spending the night in an ice-cold bath.
2. Swallowing tree toads.
3. Running four miles with two piranha fish in your shorts.

**Dr Fegg *is* in trouble. All contributions please to The Chief Scout, The Scout Hut, No. 567438, Row C. Next to Throttler Hargreaves, London, England.

SEX EDUCATION
A Revised Version by a Proper Doctor

PROPER DOCTORS
DR. J.T. RAVENSCROFT P.D.
DR. M.C.J. FYFFE-PARKER P.D.
DR. E.F. WALTERS P.D.

427 HARLEY STREET
SCUNTHORPE
LINCS.

Hello'.

Sex is a very wonderful thing. It's so wonderful, people often don't talk
about it for years on end. Some people not only don't talk about it, they don't
do it. But there's very few who don't actually think about it, at least once a
week and usually on Sundays. So it's just as well to know How To Do It. This
is called Sex Education.

The first thing you need to know about sex is where to buy the chocolates.
Once you've bought the chocolates, you'll be able to go round to her house and
give them to her and there you are. If you can't find any chocolates in your
price range, or you know she doesn't like chocolates (some hopes!), then flowers
would be a good substitute. But flowers can be very expensive, too. If you're
the girl, then of course you don't buy him chocolates or flowers - but it's
still as well to know where to buy them so you can drop a hint, such as: "Have
you seen those chocolates in Bengers' Confectionery Store?" or (if you don't
like chocolates), "Gosh! I'm glad I don't have to eat those chocolates in Bengers'
at all, especially when I prefer flowers like they have in Fish 'n' Flowers round
the corner."

Well, so much for the medical side of sex.

WHAT LOVE IS
Remember not to give her either chocolates or flowers unless you're really in
love. The way you can tell if you're really in love is to look at the price and
if you think they're too expensive and they're under £1, you're not really in
love. If you think they're too expensive and they're over £1 but still under
£1.50, then it's probably only calf-love and you should wait until you're
prepared to go to £2.50 or until the price of confectionery goes up. Anything
over £3 is love.

A WORD OF WARNING
For goodness sake Be Sensible and don't go taking any risks - such as buying
chocolates with hard centres only, when she might prefer soft centres. Take
precautions and for goodness sake, if you don't know which she prefers, buy a
selection - preferably a mixture of hard and soft centres and milk and plain
chocolates as well.

Well, that's it. Don't forget that sex is a very wonderful thing, and should
not be treated lightly (especially when most decent gift boxes can cost up to £3).
Remember, sex is also pretty expensive and can lead to stomach ache and bad teeth.

NOT PROPER DOCTORS
DR. E. WIGGLIT   DR. R. SOLE   SIR CYRIL KORWATTER-BIGGUN
KEN I.C. YORTITZ (ISRAEL)   DR. NICK URSE

SOCCER   Soccer – My Way by The Supremes

No. 11 TACKLING FROM BEHIND

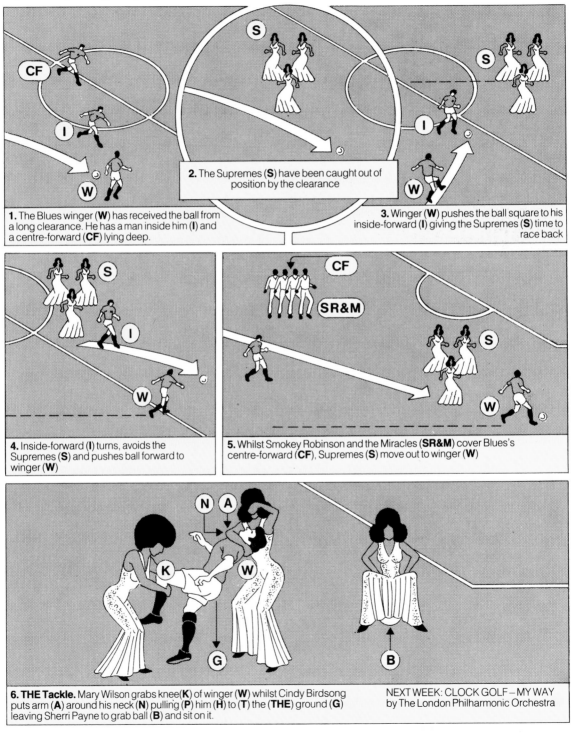

2. The Supremes (**S**) have been caught out of position by the clearance

1. The Blues winger (**W**) has received the ball from a long clearance. He has a man inside him (**I**) and a centre-forward (**CF**) lying deep.

3. Winger (**W**) pushes the ball square to his inside-forward (**I**) giving the Supremes (**S**) time to race back

4. Inside-forward (**I**) turns, avoids the Supremes (**S**) and pushes ball forward to winger (**W**)

5. Whilst Smokey Robinson and the Miracles (**SR&M**) cover Blues's centre-forward (**CF**), Supremes (**S**) move out to winger (**W**)

6. THE Tackle. Mary Wilson grabs knee(**K**) of winger (**W**) whilst Cindy Birdsong puts arm (**A**) around his neck (**N**) pulling (**P**) him (**H**) to (**T**) the (**THE**) ground (**G**) leaving Sherri Payne to grab ball (**B**) and sit on it.

NEXT WEEK: CLOCK GOLF – MY WAY by The London Philharmonic Orchestra

STICKERS (Car)

A free Fegg service. Stick one on *your* car window when visiting:

I ♥ HARE-FIELD

RANDY DOCTOR VISITING

I am a Cabinet Minister, so Sod Off!

I am a Cabinet Minister, and she is an Au Pair

I am a Cabinet Minister and he is a Private Secretary

I am a Cabinet Minister, and they are Orang-U-Tangs

I have forgotten where I parked this car

STRING

1001 Things to Do with String   1. Buy the string. 2. Tie a knot in it. 3. Tie another knot in it. 4. or 5. If it's long enough, tie a third knot in it, or, if not, untie one of the previous knots. 6. Untie any remaining knots. 7. Flick the string onto the floor with a rolled-up newspaper. 8. Throw the string away. (If you live on a farm or have relatives in politics, there are other things you can do with a string.)

TECHNOLOGY

Technology has advanced with such bewildering speed over the last few years that it is impossible to list every great breakthrough. Here are some of the most recent exciting developments of the twentieth-century:

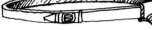

Dr Fegg's do-it-yourself teeth

A real breakthrough. Just leave these teeth on the table and they will eat your meal for you while you're out playing tennis or buying clocks. They'll brush themselves at night, and smile automatically when you're in a good mood. Need no gums or roots! Will eat anything! Do not leave near dead dogs.

The 'Tally-Ho' Automatic Bed-Wetter

A strangely pointless device, but one which has brought pleasure to thousands. Primed and placed beside the bed before retiring, the "Tally-Ho" Automatic Bed-Wetter remains crouching for a random length of time (min. three hours) after which it will suddenly spring onto the bed and wet it.

The 'Hygena' Automatic Nose Picker

Strapped to the nose in the normal way, this highly sensitive automatic device is activated by any foreign particle entering the nose. The yellow light glows, an alarm bell rings, and the extricating mechanism springs into action, removing everything in the wearer's nose within seconds, wrapping it up into a neat ball, and popping it in his mouth.

The 'Little Miracle' Boot and Shoe Adaptor

Instantly converts any article of footwear into an easily recognizable member of the Cabinet, and/or a luxury maisonette with fully-fitted kitchen and bathroom and electric night storage heaters, whichever you would prefer.

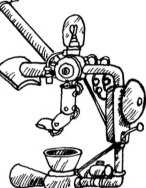

Self-Adjusting Door Knocker

Responds according to the caller. Emits sharp rapping sound for official visitors, a soft chime for intimate friends, a rude farting noise for vicars, and a strange, high-pitched whining sound for anyone not wearing underpants. For officers of the law, canvassing members of Parliament, and comedy character actors, it emits a huge spray of unpleasant slime, which will cover the caller from head to foot in a matter of seconds.

Our complete *HYGENA* range of Automatic Bodily Aids will cope with ALL bodily irritations while leaving both your hands FREE for reading or sewing.

The *HYGENA* Midget Scratcher *(for localised pruritic ailments)*

The *HYGENA* Octopus Multi-Directional Scratcher

The *HYGENA* Baldwin Trouser Extricator *(automatically and hygienically extricates trousers from between the buttocks after that long business meeting)*

The *HYGENA* Hercules Orifice Cleaner *(leaves no noticeable bulge in the clothing)*

The *HYGENA* Super Constellation de Luxe

What SATISFIED CUSTOMERS have said about the *HYGENA* range:

VIC ROGERS – voted *News Of The World* Chef of the Year 1975: "Congratulations. I was able to complete my winning soufflé while having my nose picked, my bottom scratched and my pimples burst by your Super Constellation de Luxe."

MONICA HEWLETT – *Northampton housewife:* "At last my husband and I can hold hands at the cinema again knowing that the 'Hygena' Midget is doing its valuable work underneath my jumper."

Europe on $1 a year

After many years of careful research, Dr Fegg has come up with a package deal to beat them all. No less than twenty-nine European capitals (and remember there *are* only twenty-two!) on precisely ONE dollar a year!

Places to Stay in Europe on ONE DOLLAR a Year
Paris: Main sewers (entrance in gay Montparnasse).
Rome: Auxiliary relief sewer (not open Sundays).
Zurich: The Swiss National Sewer (chairs provided).
Oslo: Den hoved kloakk (the main sewers).
Vienna: The National Museum of Austrian Science and Technology – "Sewers through the Ages" exhibition.
Frankfurt: Das Frankfurtische Hauptscheisswasser (the pretty little main drain)

For full details of this amazing Value for Money Plan, send thirty dollars and the form below to:

Fegg Enterprises,
c/o The Prison Visitor,
Greater London Council
Social Services Department,
London, England

How to Get around Europe on ONE DOLLAR a Year
A special route, known as LA ROUTE SANITAIRE, connects most of the major European capitals before flowing out into the Adriatic. Admission is through any Gentleman's Convenience, and is COMPLETELY FREE.

How to Spend Your ONE DOLLAR
Send one dollar for full details.

I would like, not free of charge, full details of Dr Fegg's Amazing Economy Plan.

WHY SO CHEAP?
Because FLY-EEZI, ("The airline that can't *afford* to crash") – offers free trips to Europe for anyone with a working knowledge of navigation or flying. FLY-EEZI take nineteen and a half days to get to Europe, but they *are* very careful. You should land at or near London Airport, but some flights, if they're going really well, may go on to Paris or even Poland.

There are two refuelling stops en route, both in New York. FLY-EEZI also run an economy flight, which takes anything up to 6 years.

EVEN CHEAPER!
Dr Fegg is experimenting with a 3,000-mile ramp and a motorbike, but at the time of writing, this is not considered a reliable method for the average traveller, owing to a slow puncture on the bike.

UNBELIEVABLE CHEAPNESS!
You should have now arrived in Europe with your *one* dollar intact. Now comes the moment

---

I enclose thirty dollars and a cake with an oxyacetylene drill inside.

NAME: ....

ADDRESS: ....

....

....

Type of Locks on Doors and Windows: .....

Best Night for Going Out: ....

Dr Fegg will personally visit you in your own home to give you the Plan. As it is valuable and confidential, Dr Fegg will place the Amazing Economy Plan in your safe, so please leave it open.

CUT HERE

---

when you can actually make a profit on your trip! Near London Airport, there are several large banks. Go into any one of these and ask for more money than you would have in your account if you had any money at all. When they refuse to give you all this money, tell them this is "a stick-up" and would they "quit fooling around." If they then hand you over all the money you asked for, get in touch with Dr Fegg immediately, and give him the name of the bank. It is more likely that they will ask you to "go away" and to "stop being silly." Do not give up. Remember your holiday in Europe is at stake. Go next door to another bank, only this time add a note of urgency to your request by pointing two Sterling submachine guns at the cashier. He will then hopefully press a bell, and within seconds the bank will be surrounded and you will be the centre of interest for several men in blue uniforms. Stick with them! They will not only give you a FREE RIDE! into London, they will also give you a FREE ROOM! for the night.

Key to Safety Features

1. Collapsible nose section (marked by arrows) to absorb impact.
2. Passenger accommodation. To provide omnidirectional cushioning passengers are suspended in these specially constructed vats of warm jelly (choice of seven flavours on all Pan-Am flights).
3. Fifty-six pilots.
4. Main torsion box (fuel tank) filled with a mixture of sugar and water – nonflammable and extremely sweet (the *only* fuel which, in the event of fire, instantly becomes jolly nice toffee).
5. Automatic puncture repair outfit. Includes sticky patches, adhesive, and a bowl of water.
6. Rear light.
7. Saddlebag.
8. Engines. Nice, safe Rolls-Royce 'Extra Safe' safety engines with special safety attachments.
9. Lifeboat.
10. Thirty-six days' provisions (including plenty of rye-crispbread for those who have to watch their waistlines).
11. Short-wave radio (can be used as auxiliary speaker for 'Speak Your Weight' machine – see No. 10).

12. Telescopic flap; waves white flag if attacked in error by the Russian Air Force.
13. Map of London underground.
14. *Lett's Pocket Diary* (with maps of the whole world in the back).
15. A letter from the Queen explaining who you are (can be filled in on landing).

16. Paddles.
17. Sunshades.
18. Suntan lotion.
19. Après suntan moisturing cream and skin conditioner.
20. Six pairs of Wellingtons.
21. Back numbers of *Which* magazine (including 'Best Buy in Gumboots', 1973).
22. Flask of hot cocoa (very sweet).
23. Flask of hot cocoa (not quite so sweet).
24. Flask of hot cocoa (unsweetened).
25. Flask of hot cocoa (even sweeter than the first one – really quite sickly).

THE MODERN BRITISH SAFETY PLANE

26. A really good jigsaw.
27. A copy of Alan Hudson's autobiography (if written).
28. 'Squelcho' evaporating fluid for over-moistened skin (see No. 19).
29. Reinforced barrier to prevent the fifty-six pilots reaching the lifeboats first.
30. West Bromley Fighting Haddock.*
31. Millet-sprays (to distract kamikaze pigeons pledged to clog Rolls-Royce 'Super Safe' safety engines with their nasty, scrawny, dirty little bodies all covered in feathers that stain and scratch the nice clean metal).

32. Armoury in case the fifty-six pilots *do* break out.
33. Moat.
34. Specially fortified toilets for last-ditch defence against the pilots, maddened by the sight of the luxurious conditions enjoyed by the passengers in the first class cabin, as compared to the overcrowded squalor of the cockpit.
35. Dungeons.
36. Special weight to prevent the plane flying above the ground.

*Should be under **Animals**

Dr FEGG's ENCYCLOPEADIA OF ALL WORLD KNO...

TERRY

Dr Fegg's Book-of-the-Month Club

CHOOSE ANY ONE OF THESE TITLES & WE WILL SEND YOU No. 56 FREE!

Hundreds of titles to choose from

GARDENING

1. Everything There Is to Know About Garden Pests
2. Garden Pests for Beginners
3. Bigger Garden Pests (No. 6)
4. You Too Can Raise Garden Pests
5. Caring for Garden Pests
6. Tropical Garden Pests in Your Own Home
7. Garden Pests over Six Feet long

ANIMAL TRAINING

16. Teach Your Dog to Foul the Footpath
17. Teaching Plankton to Sing
18. Make Your Frog Sit Up and Pay Attention
19. Make Your Cat Walk Oddly
20. Train Your Dachshund to Spit
21. Teach Your Pet Cobra Everything There Is to Know About Right and Wrong
22. Edible Pets (not exactly a training manual)
23. Pets You Should Not Eat (again, not exactly a training manual, but very necessary)
24. Pets You Shouldn't Even Antagonise (by the author of I Kicked a Bengal Tiger)

25. Teach Your Bengal Tiger to Put Others First
26. Teach Your Cobra to Coil Up Like a Table Mat and Roll onto Doris Day's Dining Room Table (not to be used in conjunction with Manual 6)

LANGUAGES

27. Learn to Speak Qjxgh
28. Qjxgh for Beginners
29. Qjxgh Made Easy
30. Simple Qjxgh
31. What Is Qjxgh?
32. Why Should Anyone Want to Speak Qjxgh?
33. Other Reasons for Speaking Qjxgh
34. Qjxgh Is My Native Language by Žkqxgh Xqgzkh
35. Qjxgh Is My Xzqgh (Advanced Qjxgh) by Ghzxc Qghzx
36. Qjxgh without Ghxzq
37. Qjxgh without Ghxzq but Not without Zqhgj by Yehudi Menuhin
38. Does Qjxgh Exist?
39. Spotting Fraudulent Languages Courses for Beginners by Inspector Potter of Scotland Yard.

HORROR

40. The Nasty Babysitter

41. I Was Barbra Streisand's Double

INSURANCE

42. Sex and Insurance
43. The Nude Insurer
44. Insuring With Three or More People
45. Insuring in the Kitchen
46. I Was a Teenage Insurance Maniac
47. The Urge to Insure
48. Insurance Without Guilt but with a Few Legal Difficulties

ADVENTURE

49. Everest – Those Difficult First Few Feet (as told to Dr Fegg)

ART

50. Great Paintings of Our Time
51. Great Paintings of Our Time and Where to See Them
52. Great Paintings of Our Time and How to Get Them out of the Frame
53. Great Warning Shouts of Our Time
54. Deafness – The Twentieth Century Problem
55. Dr Fegg's Book of Cell Improvements
56. Dr Fegg's Encyclopeadia of *All* World Knowledge

I promise to buy at least 30 books a day for the next 40 years or the duration of my natural life – whichever should be longer. Should I wish to terminate this agreement I understand I will not be able to claim damages for any action taken by Dr Fegg against me or my dependants.

☐ Yes, I wish to join Dr Fegg's Book of The Month Club and enjoy all the cultural and social benefits of a literary milieu.
☐ No. Please come and beat me up.

NAME ....
ADDRESS ....

Unidentified Flying Objects
(Scotsmen)

UFO

Throughout the 1950s and 60s, there were frequent reports of Scotsmen being sighted, sometimes quite close to heavily·populated urban areas. Many of these Scotsmen turned out to be false alarms. Often, there were quite simple explanations – they were combinations of radiation mirages and dual laser concentrations caused by ultra-violet filament distortion in the iris or common or garden supraterrestrial iodine clusters reflecting increased interorganic activity in the lower ionosphere. But

sometimes these Scotsmen weren't so easily explained away.

In 1954, Sid Tuckleberry, an unemployed illusionist, claimed to have actually spoken to a "Scotsman." "I was trying out a new pair of nail clippers in the desolate Sierra Madre Mountains in Northern New Mexico," recalls Mr Tuckleberry, "when I suddenly became aware of a presence beside me. I turned, and there in front of my very eyes was a "Scotsman" of the kind I had heard so much about. He was very much like you or me, except that he had no underwear on. He asked me if I would like to see Glasgow, and I said: 'Yes, I would.' Believe it or not, we

are now living happily together at 18b Raglan Court, Rutherglen, Glasgow 12:"

Not all sightings of these "Scotsmen" proved as happy as Mr Tuckleberry's. A Mr Vince Tuckleberry (no relation) of Dayton, Ohio, reported a sighting in December 1959. "I was in a dimly lit room, minding my own business, when I heard a strange roaring sound. It seemed to be getting nearer and nearer, until it stopped right beside me. It was definitely a Scotsman. It called me 'sonny' and asked me if that was my drink. Then it hit me."

The government and the Pentagon have repeatedly

denied using Scotsmen as secret weapons; indeed, as late as 1967, General Tuckleberry of L.I.A.R. (Limitation of International Arms Research) denied that the U.S. had Scotsmen hidden in silos deep under the Iowa countryside. "There are no such things as Scotsmen," said the General, when questioned at the Western Pentagon in Palm Springs, "and even if I were lying, we wouldn't use them."

VID

I PICKED BOGIES FROM DEAD NAZI WAR CRIMINALS' NOSES (AND ATE THEM)

Originally titled *Jour de Fête* – this is a soppy French film specially re-edited by Fegg for the Nasty label.

HORROR ON THE 19 BUS

Two late-night passengers encounter Cyril Smith on a night-service bus and have their faith in Edward du Cann shaken.

[Sorry. This should come under 'Politics'. *Ed*]

THE PHANTOM TEENAGE HEADLESS NUN OF THE OPERA GOES BERSERK IN BUCHENWALD

Very much one for those who can remember the original version with Cicely Courtneidge and Jack Hulbert.

I WAS A TOTALLY BONKERS TEENAGE PSYCHOPATH

What happens when Mr & Mrs Parker give their crazed psychopathic son Kevin a huge Black & Decker drill for Christmas.

'A must for anyone interested in carpentry.' *The Woodworker*
'A mine of useful tips for the woodworker who has taken more than enough from his parents.' *Carpentry & Horror Weekly*

I ATE THE EARS OF MEN WHO HAD CHOPPED LITTLE BABIES IN TWO (PG)

Don't be misled by the title. This is rather an affecting tale of a young boy growing up amidst the splendours of the Lake District. Beautifully photographed.

EEEURGGHHH!

Dr Fegg's Life Story, at last available on video. Starring John Mitchum, Sid Redford, Wilfred Connery and Donald Sinden.

The video revolution has changed the face of western civilization: Dr Fegg, always in the forefront of new technology, has assembled his own video library. Here is a selection of items from it which are available on VHS, Betamax or VUF (Virtually Unwatchable Feggvision). For sales and rentals write to Dr Fegg's Nasty Video Library, c/o Warder Johnson, The Grosvenor Hotel, London.

EO

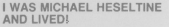

I WAS MICHAEL HESELTINE AND LIVED!

The story of a young Catholic fireman who became possessed by the body of Michael Heseltine, and his courageous struggle back to sanity.

I RAISED YOUNG NUNS TO SUCK THEIR BRAINS

A detailed account of how the rate-capping proposals were steered through Parliament.

[Sorry, 'Politics' again. *Ed*]

HOT VIDEOS

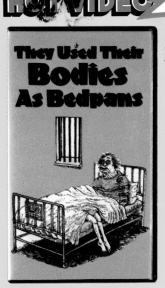

THEY USED THEIR BODIES AS BED PANS

Filmed partly in Cinemascope and partly in 8 mm, this film shows graphically what happens when a group of film producers realise they've backed the wrong project half-way through the filming.

RANDY PHILANTHROPISTS

Len tries to eat one of the most unpleasant things on earth, and gets half-way through it to the amazement of almost everyone except the dog. Vivid colour. (Money not refundable on this one.)

TABLE SEX

When lovely Lola slips it off, it smashes on the floor and Kevin treads in it.

BLACK ROD

Ethnic sex at its boldest. Filmed actually *in* Linda Chalker's office!
[Sorry. 'Politics' again.]

THE MOST HORRIBLE THINGS YOU CAN POSSIBLY IMAGINE

VOL 12: Inside the Toilets of the Punjab
In preparation:
VOL 13: Dr Kissinger.
VOL 14: Wounds of the World.
VOL 15: I Was A Teenage Rate Capper.

HEALTH

TERMINAL AEROBICS

Ease yourself into Euthanasia with Dr Fegg's stage-by-stage course to physical disintegration.

THE WORLD BETWEEN OUR TOES

A fascinating revelation of the teeming life-forms and exotic growths that exist immediately before bathtime.

THE WORLD IN OUR EARS

A fascinating revelation of the teeming life-forms and exotic growths which can be dug out with just the fingernail and a biro top.

THE WORLD UP OUR NOSE

A fascinating revelation of the teeming life-forms and exotic growths who have taken out mortgages with the Halifax.

I LIKE DYSENTERY

The frank and often touching account of how a young man found solace and escape from a hostile world in illness.

UP THE CLINIC

The story of one man's courageous fight for the right to practise gynaecology without ever getting very good at it.

VERSE

The Widow and her Otter

As sung to Dr Fegg, the well-known collector of folk songs, on the beautiful and remote island of Skye, as he was returning to the distillery.

'Twas on a dirk an' stormy nicht,
The Widow an' her otter
Were seated roun' the fire sae bricht,
When someone came an' gotter!

They wondred why? They wondred who?
They wondred how he'd hitter?
But as they wondred what to do . . .
They heard the otter titter!

It tittered once, it tittered thrice,
It rolled aroun' the floor.
It started laughing out aloud . . .
An' then it laughed some more!

It clutched its sides an' howled wi' glee!
An' the Widow? – och! They forgotter. . . .
They stood in awe . . . struck dumb to see
That helpless, laughing otter.

It shrieked wi' mirth. It split its sides . . .
The tears ran to its eyes.
An' then it stopt, an' walked awa' . . .
Much to their surprise.

An' to this dee, the folks on Skye
Say they dinna ken the half. . . .
Wha' made ol' Widow Braidie die?
Wha' made the otter laugh?

A Rabbi's Lament

A panto-writer, Harry Hyam,
Who was extremely fond of rhyme,
One day said to his comrades: "I'm
Just sick of writing pantomime
For which I get paid half a dime
I'm going to write a poem sublime,
By which you'll see my fame will climb.
Above all others, for this time
I'm only going to use ONE rhyme!"
His friends said he was past his prime
And even working overtime,
They said, he'd never keep ONE rhyme
Right through a poem. But Harry Hyam
Had started off, and by noontime
He'd written fifteen lines of rhyme
Each one the same, and by teatime
He'd written more and more betime.
But listen! Isn't it a crime?
It happened that a small enzyme*
That looked like just a speck of lime
Had landed on his hand some time,
And as he heard the midnight chime
This enzyme started making slime
That smelt of matters maritime,
And oozed out through his fingers' grime
And landed on his paper. I'm
Quite sure I do not need to mime
What happened next, but, by bedtime,
This slime and grime had caused a zyme**
Which wholly covered Harry Hyam,
And, as he lived in Hildesheim
Which has a hot and sultry clime
(Especially in the summertime),
This zyme converted into chyme***
And soon digested Harry Hyam
From slimy feet to slimey cyme, ****
His hands, his hair, his pen, his rhyme.
And all it left was half a dime
They'd paid him for the pantomime
They put on, once, in Burgwindheim.
His friends came round at breakfast time,
And sighed to find this paradigm
Of poets gone. The half a dime
They took and tied it up in sime*****
And buried it in Gundelsheim.
And on the grave they planted 'thyme',
– For that's all there was left to rhyme.

*Enzyme: Any of a class of complex organic substances that cause chemical transformations of material in plants and animals; formerly called ferment.

**Zyme: The substance causing a zymotic disease. (Zymotic: A general epithet for infectious diseases, originally because regarded as being caused by a process analogous to fermentation.)

***Chyme: The semifluid pulpy acid matter into which food is converted in the stomach by the action of the gastric secretion.

****Cyme: A head (from the French cyme or cime, meaning "top, summit").

*****Sime: A rope or chord (a northern dialect word last recorded in 1899).

Dr Fegg* writes

Laboratory experiments on men and women dressed as rats show that the outpouring of violent anger is an absolutely necessary and healthy human activity. We took six subjects randomly chosen from a white, football-playing family of Buddhist converts living in Grantham and subjected them to a succession of very hard pokes with a sharpened piece of metal. We found that after about half an hour the subjects (who were still alive) began to become restless, and irritable. Popular responses were "Stop it!", "Lay off", and even, "Hey, that hurts!".

When the pokes with the sharpened piece of metal were interspersed with heavy blows on the back of the head, the responses became more indignant—"Stop it, please!" and even "Lay off, you bastard!" from one subject. The verbal anger, which *they did not have when the experiment began*, started to increase, until one or two of them began to try and forcibly prevent our scientists from raining blows on their heads. In some cases the amount of force used was quite strong and, indeed, one of our people received a cut lip.

But as soon as they stopped the hitting and poking responses varied from being "thankful" to being "glad to be alive". This assertion of well-being demonstrates clearly the value of their anger and resistance. So, when you next feel as though "everything's going fine". . .just break a few shelves in the kitchen and throw the cat at the postman or run repeatedly at a tree with your head lowered. You'll be surprised how different you feel.

*Many people ask: What is Dr Fegg a doctor of? Well, without going into specifics Dr Fegg has tried his hand at many things in his time. His is the sort of mind that can encompass deck chair repairing, sweeping, billposting and the buying and selling of cars with one previous owner. So it is perhaps unfair and irrelevant to confine his extraordinary talents to the mundane world of labels and categories. Dr Fegg *has* delivered babies, but only during the busy pre-Christmas period when the Post Office can't cope. And Dr Fegg has done brain surgery —though *never*, repeat *never* in the Bournemouth area.

Zero-rated. The term given to items on which Value Added Tax is not payable. Mistaken Identity is one of these.

HITLER'S DOUBLE
I was

Cases of zero-rated mistaken identity are often strange but perhaps none stranger than that of Mr A. Hitler of Reigate, Surrey, the MI5 double agent whom the Gestapo used as a triple agent in what they thought was a dangerous gamble which, if they hadn't known, might have made the British think the Germans thought they didn't know they could not have known about the Scharnhorst. Here is an extract from his autobiography.

I first met Hermann Goëring, or Harry Webster of MI6 as *we* knew him, at a Nazi Youth Rally (which of course to *us* was nothing more than a front for the Reigate Young Conservatives Dance) in Düsseldorf – the code name for Dorking.

He clicked his heels together, bowed low, and asked me if I would like to lead the Nazi party. The make-up was uncanny. Harry Webster's accent was superb, his facial gestures and movements perfectly observed. Even his physical shape was the exact replica of Goëring's.

"Harry, it's *marvellous*." I whispered.

"Was ist das, mein Führer?" he exclaimed.

So brilliant was Harry Webster's disguise that we had to talk German the whole evening. He told me of his plans for invading Poland, for building up the Luftwaffe, and for replacing the ageing Hindenburg, with the help of the Ruhr industrialists. In fact, he was so good that when, at the end of the evening, I eventually said, "Harry, there's something I've got to do," and tried to pull his nose off, he shot me dead.